Jazz is Good

Dan Parrns

The Magic of Medicare 7, 8 or 9

And All That Jazz

Nancy Gilmore

SAGAMORE PUBLISHING
Champaign, IL

Production Manager: Susan M. McKinney
Cover and photo insert design: Michelle R. Dressen
Proofreaders: Phyllis L. Bannon and Nancy Gilmore

Library of Congress Catalog Card Number: 93-84241
ISBN: 0-915611-75-9

Printed in the United States.

Medicare 7, 8 or 9 tapes and compact discs are available from the
University of Illinois Alumni Association
Room 227 Illini Union
1401 W. Green
Urbana, IL 61801
217-333-1471

For my parents and my three sons, Bill, Bob and Steve.

Acknowledgments

Dan Perrino is, by all accounts, the very heart and soul of Medicare 7, 8 or 9. This book would not have been possible without his guidance, patience, and devotion in getting the story out and getting it right. My deepest appreciation to Dan and the many others—band members, fans and people in the University of Illinois family, both past and present—who helped to shape what is to follow. And, my apologies if I have overlooked or excluded anyone who has had a stake in the band's history. There are just so many of you.

Nancy Gilmore

Contents

Tributes

"For as long as most of us can remember, Medicare 7, 8 or 9 has been a delightful fixture at the University of Illinois. Wherever I turn, it seems, Medicare is there: on the Quad, in the Illini Union, in Florida, Arizona, Chicago or California.

For more than two decades, these good-time ambassadors, led by the indefatigable Dan Perrino, have charmed audiences from coast to coast. They are woven into the cultural fabric of the Urbana-Champaign campus; they are among our living icons.

Above all, Medicare 7, 8 or 9 is good music, good fun and, invariably, good cheer for all of us."

Stanley O. Ikenberry, President
University of Illinois

"They are the greatest ambassadors the University of Illinois has ever had."

That is how I have always introduced Medicare 7, 8 or 9 to alumni groups and hundreds of other organizations who enjoy good music.

The University of Illinois Alumni Association has been privileged to sponsor the band's appearances in concerts all over the United States as well as the state of Illinois. The musicians' performances generate such enthusiasm that at the end of their gigs, the audiences always clamor for more.

The Medicare band is a mix of many individuals but its leadership comes from Dan Perrino and Stan Rahn. Both men spend many hours in the alumni office before and after tours, and each musician gives above and beyond the call of duty for Illinois.

I am pleased that Medicare's 23-year history is being recorded in book form. All of us will enjoy memories of the band's past and hold good thoughts for its future as we read about one of our favorite groups."

Louis D. Liay
Executive Director and Chief Administrative Officer
University of Illinois Alumni Association

"In the 1960s, during the unrest on campuses spawned by the Vietnam War, tensions ran very high. It was then, at the height of campus tension, that Medicare was formed. The original members stepped forward to play and the students loved them.

They have been playing ever since, all over this nation, and their popularity has not diminished. They are ambassadors of good will for the Urbana campus. People love them because they love people. It's a tradition I hope never ends."

Morton W. Weir
U. of I. Chancellor at Urbana-Champaign, 1988-93

"Large universities are often known for their athletic teams, marching bands or other visible symbols composed of tens to hundreds of people. It is rare in the life of a big university that a unifying symbol emerges that all hold in high regard. In the turbulent student unrest days of the '60s, a small jazz band, called Medicare 7, 8 or 9, emerged as a conciliatory, unifying group at the University of Illinois. Because of the attitudes and the abilities of this small group of musicians, tense students and faculty who had difficulty speaking to one another loosened up and started to communicate. Medicare 7, 8 or 9 greatly improved the atmosphere of the University of Illinois.

Even though those times have passed, the ability and attitudes of this band have persisted as a wonderful, unifying force among students, faculty and alumni of the university. The Medicare group is more welcome at alumni meetings in Illinois, or indeed across the nation, than the football team, the basketball team or the marching band. The members are excellent musicians, but more than that, are excellent ambassadors for the university.

My wife, Doris, and I were privileged to get to know the members of Medicare 7, 8 or 9 during our three years at the University of Illinois, and held them in extremely high regard. I was delighted to appear on the same program with them on several occasions, even though I knew anything I said or did would come in second to their superlative performance.

The University of Illinois is extremely fortunate to have dedicated members of the university community who care so much and do so much to nurture the welfare of the faculty, students, staff and alumni of this great university."

Thomas E. Everhart
President, California Institute of Technology
U. of I. Chancellor at Urbana-Champaign, 1984-87

Foreword

"Music has charms to sooth a savage breast;
To soften rocks or bend a knotted oak."

Perhaps none of these oft-quoted words written by William Congreve in 1697 were in the minds of eight campus musicians as they gathered in the Illini Union's South Lounge November 20, 1969.

A somewhat strange conglomerate of faculty, administrators and students were on the way to perform an afternoon musical concert for whoever might show up at the Union. No rehearsals preceded, no mass publicity sought listeners, no one knew just what the outcome might be.

These were troubled times on university campuses across the nation. Thousands everywhere had marched, defied the law, engaged in physical and brutal struggles. Urbana-Champaign's campus, for so many years conservative, well-disciplined, self-regulated, had seen disruption which few seasoned faculty believed could have happened there.

Now, this small band of musicians was gathering to see if music could be the common bond that would begin a process of restoring friendship, understanding and mutual trust.

Would music be helpful? If so, what kind?

The small band elected to try Dixieland. It was to be the kind of music that would cause Louis Armstrong to exclaim when asked what it was, "Man, if you gotta ask, you'll never know."

Impetus for the concert having stemmed from the dean of students office, clearance had been sought and reluctantly given by the chancellor of the Urbana-Champaign campus. Mass gatherings were not looked upon with favor since they sometimes resulted in violence.

Nevertheless, an OK came from Vice Chancellor Jack Briscoe to Dean of Students Hugh Satterlee. Two of Satterlee's staff, Dan Perrino and Stan Rahn, were primarily involved. The gamble was on.

Few students had gathered when the band started to play as the Altgeld Hall chimes signalled 12 noon. Faculty, for the most part, shunned the South Lounge to avoid confrontation with activists. The same held true for more conservative students who came to study, not to fight.

But Dixieland music is catching! It makes you want to stamp your feet, clap your hands, sing or wiggle a dance step. It was that kind of music that poured out in the South Lounge that day.

The crowd kept gathering as the "originals" played. People liked what they were hearing. The hate, so prevalent for months, suddenly was not apparent. There were smiles on faces as Dan Perrino announced the numbers and played his saxophone. Stan Rahn played clarinet and sang.

Art Proteau picked magic notes from his banjo. John O'Connor hit high C on the trumpet. Rhythm came from the drums and Charles Braugham, Larry Dwyer added his touches on the piano keyboard while Terry Gates manufactured big sounds on the tuba.

There were not only smiles, but cheers for the band as the concert progressed. Everybody had to quit as bells rang for afternoon classes. But word was going around campus about this musical group and how everybody liked what they heard. The historic afternoon was to launch a 23-year career for "Medicare 7, 8 or 9."

The term Medicare was in deference to older musicians who were approaching retirement. The 7, 8 or 9 was explained by Perrino—"because we never did know just how many musicians we'd have on any given occasion." Later, more strict standards of qualification would prevail. But at the start, Medicare had accomplished a giant first step in its mission. Make people smile; "soothe a savage breast."

As wars have their turning point, music was to show the way to end campus unrest and protest. Music was to be a

ix

common bond that turned hatred into smiles, healed wounds of racial discrimination and resistance to the Vietnam conflict.

More than 100 musicians have climbed to the bandstand since that historic introduction of the original eight. They came from the faculty, the administration, the graduate and under-graduate student body, the alumni. Some were just good friends of the U. of I. Women, led by Karen Korsemeyer, a music major, and would lend their talents to the group.

From on-campus performances, the Medicare band ex-panded to become an ambassadorial link to alumni and to the public across the land. Medicare has played for state governors, had invitations from presidents of the United States, has ap-peared before masses of citizens in Chicago's First National Bank Plaza. It has appeared in the Rose Bowl, the Liberty Bowl and on Ft. Lauderdale's beaches at spring break.

The band's contribution has been monumental. In many ways, Dan Perrino has been throughout the spirit of Medicare. His leadership has guided appearances in more than 15 states, in more than 90 annual performances, and he is responsible for the identification and involvement of talented musicians who have created the story this book is all about.

Charles E. Flynn
University of Illinois Professor of Journalism Emeritus
Editor Emeritus, *The News-Gazette*

1

Overture

A cold wind swept over the east central Illinois prairie on that wintery December 1, 1990. Inside the magnificent Krannert Center for the Performing Arts on the University of Illinois campus, 35 musicians were heating up the Playhouse Theater for 600 faithful in the audience with their special brand of jazz.

A "sold out" sign on the marquee disappointed many more fans who had to be turned away at the door. A bummer for those who had come from miles away.

On stage, clad in their blue blazers and politically correct orange-and-blue-striped ties (Illinois' school colors), the band divided itself into four groups—brass, percussion, keyboard, and strings—sound-checking their instruments for this jazz jubilee.

The occasion marked a musical milestone for the group, which normally consisted of seven, eight or nine players, not the 35 present that day. Though it was the band's eighth appearance at the world-renowned Krannert Center, this gig was for posterity—the recording of the band's first compact disc.

Medicare 7, 8 or 9 may not engage immediate name recognition such as Dave Brubeck, Stan Kenton, George Shearing, Ella Fitzgerald, or other famed jazz and blues greats, but up to this day, this band had played nearly 2,000 performances all over Illinois and in more than 35 states across the nation. Even more astounding, it had never consciously made an effort to become organized.

With hands a-clapping and toes tapping to the rhythms, the 600 audience members, some so young they sat in their parents' laps, others whose ages more closely reflected the name of the band, and a large contingent of college students, immersed themselves in the Dixieland sound-surround.

For the next three hours, the blend of clarinets, saxophones, trombones, trumpets, banjos, pianos, drums, and vocalists raised and lowered the heartbeats in the audience with a mix of slow blues, medium tempo, and up-tempo tunes—nearly 30 in all.

"It was almost embarrassing [to play so long]," the group's leader reminisced. "I kept making all kinds of apologies [to the audience]." But he needn't have. Many who were there that day said they could have sat and listened for three more hours.

A fitting tribute to a bunch of professorial types who were perfectly convinced that their first performance, given more than 20 years previous, would also be their last.

How and why it all began is a story in itself. The longevity of the band's existence and its sustained popularity is quite another—a popularity that endears it and its individual members to young and old, all races and creeds, not only amid the cornfields of Illinois' heartland, but all over the land!

They've played for school children, state governors and senators, university officials, faculty and alumni, and just plain folks. They've played at sports events, in churches, and at funerals. They've entertained thousands across the state of Illinois and across the nation in formal concerts and informal gatherings. They've produced three public television shows, recorded seven albums, and performed on an aircraft carrier and at Disneyland.

Medicare 7, 8 or 9 is not just a band, say its originators. "It is a concept."

2

Downbeat

"*I am unable to forecast the year ahead with the same sureness that I felt in other years. This very fact is a sign of the turmoil and the instability of our times, not just in the academic world but in our country as a whole and, indeed, in our world. Our reluctance to forecast may be seen as a measure of the distractions which confront us— distractions which divert our time and energy from orderly planning and positive and creative effort. The universities today are at the vortex of a social storm. They are pulled and hauled from all sides, from the radical left, from the radical right, and from the backlash on both of these. As the agents of the extreme try to 'radicalize' students, the latter in turn seek to use the universities as the agents of the 'reforms' as defined by them.*"

David D. Henry, President
University of Illinois
September 1968

The turbulent '60s— a decade fraught with unrest. Americans wrestled with their consciences and their biases over the civil rights debate. Women's Lib was on the springboard—a movement some were convinced was long overdue. There were peace-niks, Hippies, and the mellowing out at Woodstock. There was the shame of the Kent State massacre. And hovering like a stench over the whole genre was the Vietnam War.

The political upheaval and events of the times raised the social consciousness of Americans everywhere. Perhaps it was never more evident, in terms of frustration, than in the sit-ins, demonstrations, and riots on the nation's college campuses.

A headmaster of a private school in New York and former administrator at Columbia University, Donald Barr, wrote in a *McCalls* magazine article in October 1969,

> "The rebellion that parents are financing is not one revolution, but three. The first is political . . . carried on by New Left students who want to change not only the university, but society. The second is racial. It is organized by black militants who are tired of asking for a little share and are going to take a big share of Whitey's good life and education. The third revolution is the personal revolt against reason, which embraces superstition, fate, mysticism, hippiness, and a dreadful, mindless dabbling in drugs.
>
> "On the day that parents stop paying tuition for noneducation; on the day they stop handing out allowances for strike funds and narcotics and reeking apartments, the student revolutions—impatient with reason, violent against restraint, a holiday from self-control—will wither away."

The scenes of unrest, discontent, and disruption that appeared all over the country were no different at the University of Illinois, smack in the middle of corn country. Students were angry, and they demanded change.

 za.

U. of I. Associate Dean of Students Willard Broom was a junior in the College of Communications in the fall of 1969. He remembers those days as "a time of great tension . . . the tension surrounding the Vietnam War, the civil rights movement, and the emergence of the black militant movement."

On the Urbana campus, students and administrators wrangled over how much of a role the student body should play in the governing process of the university, and that produced an even greater atmosphere of tension. "On a college campus, that translates into students versus faculty and staff.

"We were on the cusp of going from the old way of doing business to creating a new way of doing business," said Broom, who reminisced in his third-floor office of the Student Services Building on John Street in early March 1992.

"The tension was between the guardians of the old and the vanguard of the new. It got played out in the popular media as the 'generation gap.'"

But there was nothing playful about the mood of many student radicals who were highly organized and, at times, highly volatile. Though Broom will admit he took part in some of the marches during this era, he was not part of the groups who would almost routinely throw bricks through the windows of classroom and administration buildings.

"Those kinds of destructive protests began in the spring of 1970," said Broom. "We saw sit-ins and protests as part of that," but the brick-throwing resulted in "all of the windows on Green Street in Campustown and the windows in the Administration Building (on Wright Street), the English Building, which was then the chancellor's office, and the Armory being boarded up. They got broken so quickly that they just put plywood up."

Hugh Satterlee, university omsbudsman, was dean of students at the time . . . a part of the establishment students were at odds with. His memories, too, reflect the turmoil on the campus as well as the administration's attempts to deal with the various student factions, all of which had different agendas, he said.

There was the anti-war group, the student power faction, which demanded more influence and governing authority, and the black power movement "which had an entirely different agenda" than the others—they wanted to increase their numbers among the student body, said Satterlee.

But there was one man in the faculty midst who stood out. A professor of music, Dan Perrino, who was dean of student programs during this period. "He got involved in dealing with all three groups in terms of supporting elements of programming that they wanted and trying to do a number of different activities that might direct what they were trying to do and, perhaps, change the direction of what they were trying to do."

What was truly remarkable about this good-natured and concerned member of the "establishment," was that Perrino seemed to be the only one able to walk the fine line between the student body and the administration.

"Dan really seldom had any ulterior motives, and that was one of the big differences," said Satterlee. "Of all the administrators on campus, Dan Perrino was probably the only one that people totally trusted because he had no agendas," Satterlee said.

At the time, Broom worked as a student "office boy. . . a go-fer" in Perrino's office of student programs. "I ran a lot of errands for Dan." Broom also recalled that "there were only a handful of people on this campus who were able to talk to both students and faculty and staff, and one of those people was Dan Perrino.

"He would be going to a meeting at the (Illini) Union, and I'd be going with him because he needed me to carry something. But it would take us a half an hour to walk the two blocks from here [the student services building] to there because he knew everybody.

"We'd be walking over there, and a long-haired political leader would stop to talk to him, a gray-haired faculty member, the editor of the student newspaper . . . I just remember thinking, 'This is utterly amazing,' because the divisions were clear, and Dan was middle-aged and he was talking to everybody."

Even if students wanted to stage a protest, "Dan would find them a public address system. He wasn't concerned about what they would say or do or profess to do. There was no question that he was the best-liked administrator that I knew of," said Satterlee, "bar none."

He was everyone's friend "and he was trying desperately to do something to enhance the black student programming and give them some kind of outlet," said Satterlee. "The feeling on campus was that we were at odds most of the time, particularly at night. The evening hours were usually turned over to some kind of a protest march." He recalled that there was absolutely no dialog taking place between the students and the administrators.

This was where Perrino came in. "I think," said Satterlee, "that Dan was seeking different ways and means of providing some kind of common ground, a common interest to show that there was not this huge gap between generations, but the gap might have been between ideologies, and perhaps ideologies were not the more important things in the world."

Broom remembers the speaking forums on the campus that Perrino started. The program was called Campus Dialog. "The office owned a little sound system that was allegedly portable," he laughed, "kinda port-a-crib size. And when we had these dialogs, I'd lug the sound system over and set it up and run it."

Satterlee said no one in the administration really wanted to be involved in the dialogs because "the ground rules were always changed by the students or the group that we were trying to work with."

"I was involved in one of these Campus Dialogs and was asked to come over to the Union and talk about some administrative policy. When I got there I found that the students who were supposed to be debating, though it really wasn't a debate, were not there. Instead there were two faculty members . . . Lou Gold and another political scientist who was one of the most violent anti-war people (on the faculty). Essentially, what happened is that they attacked me. That is why administrators did not care to participate too much because the rules or procedures were described in one way, but by the time you got there, they had changed them.

"The dialogs really turned out to be just another platform for the radical faculty or student dissidents to promote their positions. This wasn't Dan's fault, it was just that he couldn't control it," said Satterlee.

ॐ

It was in this hostile atmosphere on November 20, 1969, that something magical happened that would "soothe the savage breast" of young campus radicals and help ease the tension among students, faculty, and administrators. It was the birth of Medicare 7, 8 or 9, though they did not know that was to be their name. That would come a little later.

Perrino told Satterlee a week before that he would like to try something different . . . something he called a "Dixieland Dialog."

In those days, the South Lounge of the Illini Union—a Georgian red brick, four-story, white-pillared building that was the gateway to the main campus and the landmark that anchored the north side of an enormous, grassy quadrangle, known as the Quad—was the gathering place for discussion, mainly for students, and particularly during the noon hour.

It was in the South Lounge that Perrino's Campus Dialog programs were held, sometimes on a weekly basis. Broom remembers a group of people that would regularly check into the Union at lunchtime to see what was going on . . . what issue or topic of the day was being discussed. The very fact that the Union was a focal point for students, faculty, and staff alike, "by virtue of all the foot traffic, people wandering by and the usual loiterers, there were at least 30 or 40 people in the South Lounge on any given day."

The South Lounge was the spot where students would "perform their verbal attacks and castigation of the administration," said Satterlee. And it didn't matter if it was the campus administration or the national one.

ã

Perrino recalled attending most of the dialog programs in the Union. He said he happened to be watching one on a particular day when fellow music professor John O'Connor came strolling by, stopped to chat and asked, "How are things going?" Perrino said he responded with something like, "OK, I guess, but there's still tension between the students and the faculty.

"I guess I was naive for thinking a change would take place overnight. How silly of me. John said, whether jokingly or not, 'What you need here is some jazz.'

"That night I thought about it over and over again. I called him the next morning to ask if he knew some musicians who might play. So, after we brainstormed together, we came up with a list of eight, including me.

"Now, I hadn't played jazz in years. As a matter of fact, I had sold all my instruments, and if I was to perform with this group, I would have to borrow an instrument. So I called each of the guys to explain to them what we were going to try to accomplish. Believe it or not, everyone was game to try."

But before Perrino could begin to organize his jazz program, he needed permission from a wary university administration official. Jack Briscoe, a professor of civil engineering, had been doing double duty as the vice chancellor for administrative affairs. Since security on campus was part of his job, Perrino had to pass muster with Briscoe.

Perrino told Briscoe, "We're just gonna have a little concert in the South Lounge." Later, Briscoe instantly recalled his reaction. "Over my dead body you're gonna have a concert," he said he told Perrino, and the two argued back and forth before an agreement was finally made.

"I was concerned," said Briscoe, "because whenever we got 10 to 12 students together outside the classroom, there was always the possibility of some kind of trouble and it gave (Chancellor Jack) Peltason and me the jitters."

When Briscoe told Perrino the only way he'd allow the concert was by placing plainclothes policemen in the area, "He about had a fit," Briscoe laughed. "It sure wasn't any secret to anyone who was there that day, either . . . the plainclothesmen stood out like sore thumbs with their short hair." (Long hair was the vogue of the day).

Perrino and the other seven of his fellow professorial members and grad students, with no rehearsal and a list of tunes, hauled their horns, drums, and other instruments over to the South Lounge on that 20th day of November for their experiment in jazz—a new kind of dialog. That they were all musicians, and darn good ones, was probably the biggest surprise of all to the audience.

Perrino on baritone sax; professors of music Morris (Mo) Carter (trombone) and John O'Connor (trumpet); student affairs administrator Stan Rahn (clarinet); director of extension, Northern District of Illinois, Art Proteau (banjo); and graduate students Terry Gates (tuba), Larry Dwyer (piano), and Charlie Braugham (drums) were the heart of what would become known as Medicare 7, 8 or 9.

Broom, who was used to hauling the "port-a-crib" sound system all over campus for Perrino's programs, was faced with an entirely new challenge. The fact that many administrators and security personnel shuddered at any gathering of 10 or more people in one spot for fear a riot would break out, did not enter Broom's mind at the time. He was used to flipping a switch to turn on the microphone for one speaker and then just sitting back in his chair. Now he was "spinning dials" frantically trying to adjust sound levels for eight musical instruments, following the "turn it up, turn it down" gestures of Perrino, the band's leader.

The mood of those present in the lounge at the time was a concern. "When Dan and his crew came over and set up, there was some resentment on the part of the students," said Satterlee. This was their turf and who was this coming in and taking over their place?

As the group began to play "really good music," said Broom, people who were just wandering by—faculty and staff—stopped to listen. The younger people were used to hearing the Rolling Stones, Jefferson Airplane or Jimi Hendrix. They didn't know what to make of this new sound. But the older people stopped because it was "their" music, "their" sound—Dixieland. "Here you had this room full of people and, for once, no one was yelling at each other," said Broom.

Perrino remembered watching the numbers in the audience begin to increase from about 75 dubious students to a standing-room-only crowd of 500. As the happy music continued, scowls turned to grins of pleasure and rhythmic clapping and applause filled the room. "Even though the audience was predominantly faculty and staff, the students' attitude eventually was sort of 'That wasn't so bad after all,'" said Satterlee.

"It was a happening! Everybody was amazed. My gosh, Stan Rahn can sing and play. They knew Mo Carter played trombone, but not that well. Dan, a saxophonist? Not really! And Art Proteau, the senior member of the group . . . He's some banjo player. Not only were these recognizable faculty faces, but they were real musicians."

Broom also was stunned. "I was amazed that here were these men, most of whom I knew as professors or administrators, and here was a side of them I had never seen."

Satterlee's reaction after that first performance, as he walked up to Perrino, was to say to him, "My God, you guys are great! Who would ever have thought that we could expect that kind of performance? I was almost worried a little about being embarrassed, thinking, 'What can these old codgers do?'"

What became an even bigger surprise, besides the fact the group had never rehearsed the performance, was that this one-time dialog would be the beginning of a 23-year relationship—between the performers, the students then and now, the university community, alumni, the local community, and so-called strangers nationwide.

When a student reporter walked up to Perrino after the performance that special day in November 1969 and asked him, "How many in your group?," Perrino replied, "It's not *my* group, and there were seven, eight or nine, depending on how many showed up." The same reporter then went over to Rahn to ask about the name of the group, and Rahn shook his head, smiled in a bemused sort of way and said, "Well, I guess considering our ages and however many of us show up to play, you could probably call us Medicare 7, 8 or 9."

About an hour after the band's performance, Perrino returned to his campus office and his secretary, Susan Spicer, said, "You've got 16 requests to play again."

The next day in *The Daily Illini*, the student newspaper, there was a picture of the band labeled "Medicare 7, 8 or 9 performs for students in the South Lounge."

No one knew, not even the members of the band, that this would be the start of something almost legendary.

3

Upbeat

The invitations to play started rolling in almost immediately after that first performance in the Union. They came mostly from student housing groups—residence halls, fraternities, and sororities. Also, at Associate Chancellor Lloyd Berry's request, the band continued its performances in the Union with some degree of regularity.

Then-Chancellor Jack Peltason, who is now president of the University of California's nine-campus system, was also, and still is, one of the band's most ardent supporters. He is one of only three "honorary" members of the band, the others being Tom Everhart, chancellor at the U. of I. from 1983-87 and current president of Caltech, and Bob Berdahl, former U. of I. administrator and now president of the University of Texas at Austin. The plaque the band gave to Peltason when he left the university now hangs on his presidential wall at Cal-Berkeley.

"Medicare was one of the few things that kept the whole campus united at a time of great turmoil," Peltason said in a 1992 phone interview. "They closed the generation gap, they closed the town and gown gap, they closed the racial gap, and they represented something around which all of the above could rally and unite."

For those very reasons, he threw his support as campus administrator behind their efforts both in front of the microphone during concerts "and behind the mike," he said. "They became one of the traditions of the university, like Chief Illiniwek, and are beloved to generations of Illini."

Of all the university administrators trying to deal with the day-to-day running of an institution of higher learning and cope with the mayhem of disruption at every turn, Peltason was regarded as the equalizer.

Willard Broom's recollections about the early days include what he called the Dad's Day gigs on campus during a football weekend each fall when students invited their fathers for three days of fun and camaraderie.

"Someone would put a notice in the Dad's Day newsletter, 'Bring your horns to campus,' and all these dads would come to the Thunderbird or Levis Faculty Center and wipe the dust off their cases and pull out their horns . . . and some were God-awful," he laughed, "but they had fun."

"Dan would lead the audience in clapping after each solo. And whether it was John O'Connor playing 'Sugar Blues' or some dad screwing up some song because he hadn't played in 10, 15, or 30 years, he would get his share of the applause. And they would jam over at the T-Bird or Levis until the place closed down.

"Some guys would come in and play the piano . . . it was a real inclusive presentation of the music. You just felt welcome. I remember setting it up one time and Dan wasn't there. He came in later and was not happy with the position of the audience. So I had to move everything forward, way forward, because he wanted the audience surrounding the group. He felt intimacy was critical in communicating with them."

Very early on, the university's Alumni Association got involved. Jim Vermette, who was the association's executive director at the time and, at age 28, fairly fresh out of college himself, remembered standing around listening to the first half dozen of the band's performances in the Union and thinking what a great alumni program the band would make "because I could see they could really communicate."

"I just went for my own personal enjoyment at first," Vermette said, "and to people-watch because there was such tension on campus in those days and you never knew when a gathering that started out peacefully would end up with some kind of violence.

"There wasn't much real communication going on between the various age groups—the faculty, staff, and the students. There was a definite generation gap, and being rather young as an executive director of the Alumni Association, I felt I had a foot in both camps.

"You'd see other people who were very rational and solid, trying to communicate, but the students wouldn't listen. Then Medicare came along and here were all these groups who had been and were so suspicious of one another clapping their hands and enjoying a real experience together."

Vermette actually had two motives on his Medicare agenda—a new and exciting program for alumni and a possible tie-in for his wife, Dena. "I knew she could sing and would fit right in."

"I remember very distinctly when I talked to Dan about Dena. It was in the north lounge of the Union, just outside of the reception area after that first concert. Dena was with me, and I introduced her to Dan saying, 'I think sometime you should hear Dena; she's been singing since college.' And Dan looked at her and asked if she would be interested, and she said she'd love it."

That brief encounter would launch a 20-plus-year career for Dena Vermette as one of Medicare's primary vocalists.

At the same time, Vermette was pitching the idea of using the band for alumni programs away from the campus. Dan told him, "Ah, Jim, we're lucky to even get a group together. We don't know who is going to show up. We just meant to do this once or twice, kinda informally."

"He thought it was a good idea," said Vermette, "but he wasn't quite sure how to engineer it.

"I had been going out trying to present to alumni a fair picture of what was happening on the campus. For the most part I thought the administration had done a very good job during a very tough time. But some alumni, really a small group of people, just could not be reasoned with and were very vocal.

"The same thing was true on campus, and I kept thinking, 'We've got to get these people together.'" After hearing Medicare perform and seeing how they appealed to students and faculty alike, he decided their style of communication, through music, would achieve the same results in the alumni ranks.

Vermette met with Peltason, and they both agreed that Medicare was something special. "He said, 'Let's work out some kind of mutual funding arrangement to send the band out on the road," Vermette said. "It's expensive when you send a group out around the state and around the country." And so the money to accomplish such tours was funded for many years by the U. of I. Foundation, the chancellor's office, the Alumni Association, and local alumni clubs.

"When Medicare appeared, everyone would leave smiling, happy and thinking positive thoughts about the university," Vermette said. "At every concert I've ever attended, at least several hundred, there has been a spontaneous standing ovation, so if that's not a form of greatness, I don't know what is."

≈

In the spring of 1970, security chief Jack Briscoe wasn't a whole lot more enthused about a Medicare concert on the campus Quad than he was about the first gig in the South Lounge of the Union. But he figured if it were held outside, buildings were in less danger of being trashed than if it were held indoors.

But Medicare's popularity was starting to grow, and the band's ability to bring so-called warring factions together was, by now, a foregone conclusion. And so permission was granted, and the band gave its first performance on the Quad in front of a crowd of nearly 7,000 students.

"A variety of groups played from 5 p.m. until 2 in the morning," Perrino recalled. Besides Medicare, there were rock, soul, and folk groups. One folk quartet, called the Bethel New Tabernacle Drive-In Church ensemble, was made up of three faculty members and a graduate student. Art professor Doyle Moore played a bonafide autoharp, political science professor Dave Wisnant played guitar, English professor James Hurt was on string bass, and the student also played guitar.

Medicare's performance was one of the highlights, and Perrino said they ended with what is now their trademark playing of "When the Saints Go Marching In." "We marched down from the steps of the Auditorium out into the crowd of these thousands of students who started marching with us . . . it was an exhilarating experience."

He said he remembered that particular concert for several other reasons. For one thing, it was the first time any person outside of the regular group played with the band. "This kid was walking by, carrying his trombone, and stopped to listen. His name was Bob Samborski and, unbeknownst to us at the time, he was in the U. of I. Jazz Band. He asked us if anyone could sit in, and we said, 'Sure, come on up.'

"This kid had never played Dixieland before, but he had a terrific ear for music. And after the first few bars of a blues melody were played, he started to improvise. He was really terrific."

Little did the regular players know that Samborski's appearance would set a trend that would perpetuate itself through the years. To date, more than 100 men and women, young and old, professional musicians, faculty, students, alumni, and others have picked up an instrument and joined in the jam sessions.

In the fall of 1970 at the first Dads' Night Out performance, another student, Eric Schneider, a business major, joined the group. He played clarinet and saxophone with Medicare on several occasions afterward and went on to distinguish himself, not in the world's trade markets or on Wall Street, but as an accomplished professional musician playing with big bands and such jazz greats as Earl "Fatha" Hines.

Another reason the first Quad concert was so memorable, said Perrino, was because of the detritus 7,000 people leave behind. "After we finally quit playing in the wee hours of the morning, I asked the crowd to be good and pick up their trash. Then we all went home. But a few hours later I got a call at home from university police officer Roger Armstrong who told me, 'Come out here. This place looks like a dump.'"

There were beer bottles and whiskey bottles and all kinds of trash all over the Quad, said Perrino. The university's board of trustees was going to be meeting that morning and no one wanted them to see the mess. "This Sgt. Armstrong called the university's physical plant people and got the maintenance crew to clean it all up before the trustees' meeting. It was a close shave, but we managed to put the Quad in its original form by 9 the next morning when the trustees' meeting began."

Perrino also remembers associating that first performance on the Quad with the first performance in the Illini Union. "There was a similar sort of attitude that we didn't do anything to bring a crowd together that would develop into a negative thing, but rather a positive thing. I wish I could say we planned it that way, but we didn't. It just kind of happened. We didn't even think about it. Everybody seemed to be enjoying themselves and there were smiles on their faces and they were concentrating on what we were doing and saying, and it just worked out.

"We were not a threat to anyone. We didn't represent one side or another or profess to have answers to issues. It was just a complete diversion and the response to the happy, lighthearted music diverted their attention, and this was very much a surprise to us."

That summer, the band received more invitations to play. They performed poolside at IMPE (Intramural Physical Education Building), and when fall arrived, moved into the area around Memorial Stadium and began entertaining fans at tailgate parties before home football games.

"That started our appearances with the Marching Illini band as part of the halftime shows," which came about through the initiative of Bill Everett, then dean of the College of Engineering, and legendary football coach Ray Eliot," said Perrino.

As things progressed, they also were invited to work their magic on the crowds when the Chicago Bears and the then-St. Louis Cardinals played an exhibition game at Memorial Stadium. Before long, they were playing at Illinois basketball games and later playing between innings at Cubs baseball games at Wrigley Field in Chicago, outings planned by the Alumni Association.

There was a fly in the ointment, however. When the musician's union got wind of these non-paid guys muscling in on their territory, Medicare was no longer welcome to play at Wrigley, and the union hired its own group to steal the U. of I. band's thunder.

Back on campus in the fall of 1970, a fully organized event called Quad Day was established. It was meant to fulfill a number of requirements—welcome new students coming to campus for the first time and make them feel a part of the university community; have a barrel of fun; and most of all, try to keep the peace by integrating the administrators and faculty with the student body and openly displaying the human connection between the two. A tough task, but it worked, and has every fall since then.

Willard Broom remembers, "It was Dan's idea to have Medicare be a part of it. I was very aware that there was a lot of objection to such a performance. There were a lot of people who didn't want him to do Quad Day—out of the chancellor's office, you know, those higher-ups." And rightly so, reminded Perrino. "The administration was still apprehensive about bringing large groups of students together for fear of another demonstration."

"I went over to the space office to reserve the space for the band," Broom recalled, "and they said, 'Oh, no, you can't do that,' and the next thing I know, after I said to Dan, 'They're not going to let us use the Quad,' we had it. How that happened, I'll never know. This guy, Pat Flynn I think his name was, was in the space office and whenever you wanted to reserve space for something other than a class, he was the guy you talked to. I think he was an old Marine, and he just said, 'no.' But the next thing I know, we had the space, and I'm trying to explain to him what we were trying to accomplish—that this was Dan's idea, and this is what I was trying to put together. The more he and I worked on it, the more he became a real supporter."

Other supporters included John Corker, who was associate director of the Illini Union at the time, Ken Allen, a founder of VIP (Volunteer Illini Projects) and students Broom and Mark Herriott.

Perrino remembers the university being able to attract political leaders from Springfield for the event such as recent U.S. Secretary of Agriculture Ed Madigan. "Students set up booths around the Quad displaying informative material on their organizations while Ben McGuire of the Division of Campus Recreation and some of his assistants arranged for games to be played— volleyball, frisbee tossing, races, etc. The focus was on fun, communication, and listening to a variety of entertainment."

That first Quad Day performance by the band stands out in Dena Vermette's mind. She described it as being "like a huge variety show" in front of thousands of people. There was a lot of talent involved at the time, and Dan was kinda testing the waters to see who would fit in with the band."

The variety show atmosphere was a solid hit. The "untouchable" establishment types—administrators and faculty, melted in with the happy mood. "John Scouffas, who was the discipline guy, the bad guy in the students' eyes," Broom recalled, "happened to be an old opera singer, and he got up and sang 'Granada' and, wow, the students reacted with cheers of 'Bravo, bravo.'"

Perrino also remembered Ray Perlman, a professor in the School of Art and Design, singing nautical songs.

"During the afternoon, Peltason was doing yo-yo tricks in a contest, and Jeff Humphrey from the financial aid office, sang and Ross Martin, associate dean of engineering, played the gosh darn wash bucket."

In fact, the yo-yo competition was one of the highlights of the day with Peltason doing the challenging. It seems he was the yo-yo champion in his sixth grade elementary class in St. Louis. Taking up Peltason's challenge was another senior administrator, Jack McKenzie, then dean of the College of Fine and Applied Arts. The two yo-yo pros so wowed the student audience that the initial Quad Day challenge became somewhat of an annual event with McKenzie being the overall winner, Perrino recalled. His pièce de résistance was using four yo-yos at one time, which really sent the audience into orbit.

Both students and faculty members at the time remember particularly a volleyball game arranged between a group of administrators and student government players. It was still a war zone between the two factions, but Jack Briscoe decided some tension relief was in order. Subterfuge or not, he arranged a one-day, zero-time appointment in the vice chancellor's office for Nick Witherspoon, a 6'8" star Illini basketball player, to be a ringer for the staff team.

"Of course, the students thought the administration was cheating and got pretty upset," laughed Broom. "But Jack hauled out the appointment papers to prove that it was all legitimate, and Witherspoon played with the administrators for a few minutes and scored a few points before being benched, just to prove that it was all in good fun."

4

On the Road

Medicare 7, 8 or 9 has taken its show on the road from the heartland of Illinois to the far corners of the nation. With the band's popularity growing with every performance in and around the university, and having tested the waters at alumni gatherings in various towns around the state, then-Alumni Association director Jim Vermette and members of the university administration recognized that these musical ambassadors were destined for greater things. In 1973, the decision was made to jointly fund the band's first out-of-state tour—to sunny California, home to a large contingent of former Illini.

Dan Perrino, Stan Rahn, John O'Connor, Morgan Powell, Dan Perantoni, Art Proteau, Bob Parkinson, Rudy James, the late Dick Cisne, ragtime pianist Ron Riddle and a bevy of spouses and assorted band instruments took to the air from Champaign to Chicago and on to San Diego.

Rahn's wife, Josie, kept a running patter of dialogue in a diary of this momentous first. It was March 22, and the day began at 4:30 a.m. for the Rahns and similar ungodly hours for the rest. None of them would sleep again for 24 hours.

"I fixed breakfast," Josie wrote, "and we got ourselves together. Danny and Marge (Perrino) picked us up right on the dot of 6 a.m., then on to the airport to meet our crew. Everybody assembled, boarded the plane for a nice, quick ride to Chicago, coffee in the airport and then to United for our flight to San Diego.

"What a beautiful flight—clear as a bell. We saw the Rockies. Wow! What a pile of rocks," she quipped.

The first order of business after landing in San Diego was a scheduled performance aboard a U.S. aircraft carrier, arranged by alumnus Navy Lt. Joe Rank.

"The Navy met us," diarist Josie wrote. "We got our rental cars, loaded all our gear, piled into the cars and started out for the San Diego Navy yards." Josie, husband Stan, Perantoni and Powell rode together in a Navy truck, and promptly got lost, taking an unscheduled tour of the famous San Diego Zoo before getting back on track.

After a flurry of saluting as they boarded the ship, the celebrities were treated to coffee in the officers' quarters and then escorted to the hangar deck where they performed for an enthusiastic bunch of sailors. A grand tour of the ship followed, and the captain sent the little group away with commemorative hats, photos, and more saluting.

After dinner and another performance, this time for a group of local alumni at Caesar's Palace, the wild and crazy jaunt continued with a 125-mile drive to Anaheim for a date at Disneyland.

The group, by this time admittedly "dead beat," was driving two vans, loaded with 17 people and piled high with band instruments tied with rope to the tops of the vehicles.

"John and (wife) Erma Jean went to Montgomery Ward, bought rope and a knife at midnight. There we are out in front of this plush restaurant, tying 40 pieces of luggage on top of the vans," Josie wrote. "We looked like we were straight out of the 'Grapes of Wrath,'" laughed O'Connor, recalling the incident 23 years later.

At 2 a.m. California time, 4 a.m. Illinois time, the little caravan arrived safe but bushed in Anaheim.

Early the next day, Perrino and Powell were strolling down the street, taking in the morning air, trying to revive themselves from the previous 24-hour ordeal. Spotting the Grand Hotel, where the band was scheduled to play that evening, Perrino decided to drop in and check out the hotel's piano. Now, anyone who knows Perrino is aware that piano-checking is a ritual anytime and anywhere the band is to perform. They can haul basses, saxes, trumpets and drums, but pianos, no. And if they're not in tune, somebody is going to pay the piper—in this case, Perrino.

Perrino recalled that prior to the trip west, he had talked several times to the assistant manager of the hotel about the piano and was consistently assured there would be no problem since the hotel had four of them. When Perrino's white-glove check came into play, however, it was a whole different story, and he was furious because not only was it "terribly out of tune, the best one they had had seven broken keys."

Ron Riddle, a former U. of I. faculty member living in the area at the time, and "a great ragtime piano player," Perrino said, was going to play with Medicare that evening. The story goes that when he arrived, he tuned the piano as best he could with a tuning fork he always carries with him. During the performance, Riddle purposely played on the broken keys and smiled impishly, sending the audience into fits of laughter because they knew he was mimicking. This infuriated the hotel's assistant manager who discovered, after the band had left, that Riddle had summarily taken his little tuning fork and untuned the piano, leaving it just as he found it.

The next performance on the agenda was a date at Disneyland, which had been arranged by O'Connor. James Christianson, manager of entertainment at the world-famous park, had at one time taught music in the public school system with O'Connor. When Christianson learned, through his friend, that the band was going to be in Anaheim, he got them an invitation to play at the Music Educators National Conference being held at the park at the time. Dixieland jazz at its finest poured out of the park's French Market restaurant that night. Medicare took turns playing with the park's regular band, and the evening ended with a combined and rousing rendition of "When the Saints Go Marching In." The crowd was so enthusiastic, wrote Josie Rahn, that they didn't get "out of there until midnight."

After several days in and around Disneyland, the little group flew to San Francisco for the next leg of the tour. But not before a few snafus. Josie wrote, "What a screwy trip! We were up very early—6:15 a.m., finished packing, had breakfast, and met everyone at 7:30 a.m. We caught the airport bus at the Disneyland Hotel, but the bus broke down and we had to change buses. When we arrived at the airport ticket counter, John (O'Connor) discovered his ticket to San Francisco had been torn out in Chicago, but they finally let him on."

It was in the Bay Area that the band encountered one of the largest crowds they had had to date. A program had been set up by the San Jose alumni club to play in the Spaghetti Factory restaurant in downtown San Jose. Regular customers and some groups from nearby universities—Santa Clara and San Jose—were in and around the restaurant that evening. "They all started to come in when they heard us playing," Perrino recalled. "It got so crowded they were practically standing on top of us. Somebody asked if we would play one of their school songs, which we did, and pretty soon everyone was requesting. We kept on playing and all of a sudden, jugs of wine were placed around us. The piano was just loaded; you would have thought it was the bar!"

Four former U. of I. musicians who lived in the area—Carl Leach, John Rinaldo, Reiber Hovde, and Jim Whiteside, joined in the performance. "It was a magic night," Rahn remembered. "Different schools, regular townspeople, alumni—the U. of I. really made a name for itself that night."

Normally, when the band takes to the road, they pack their "uniforms"—standard blue blazers, orange-and-blue-striped ties, etc.—but on the first California trip, there were no uniforms.

Perrino decided they needed to make some kind of fashion statement, so he contacted director of athletics Cecil Coleman at the university to see if the band could borrow some orange sport jackets that members of the football team wore for special occasions. A deal was struck, except for Perrino, whose stature at 5' 4" is so small a coat couldn't be found that would fit him. And, though football players are traditionally hunksters, they also had a hard time finding one big enough to fit the 6' 3", 250-pound frame of Bob Parkinson. "We ended up going to Dave Downey, a very tall, star basketball player, and ended up with a 46 long-long-long for Bob. We had the coat with us and before the performance, we were all sitting around in the hotel room in Anaheim, having some drinks, and Stan asked me to put this coat on. It came down to my ankles, and everybody just howled."

ᕦ

All the trips and tours the band has made over the years are memorable, say its members— some more so than others.

Probably the smallest audience the band ever played for was in Towson, Maryland, a suburb of Baltimore, in 1976. The gig was to be at the Towson Country Club for area alumni. When the band arrived for the performance, the number of people on hand to greet them could have been counted on one hand. It seems the president of the alumni club had forgotten to tell people Medicare was coming. So, after hastily making a bunch of phone calls, 17 finally showed up. "At first, we were disappointed with the numbers," Perrino said. "But it turned out to be one of the best times we ever had because there was so much camaraderie with our audience.

"It was a fun evening. There was no time table established, which made it much more informal, and it was like being with family." They later learned, after returning to campus, that one of the audience members made a significant contribution to the university's Foundation after the performance.

One trip they all remembered was the almost ill-fated one to Florida in 1984. The band was slated to play for a number of alumni clubs, making a swing from Washington, D.C., and Atlanta, to Ft. Lauderdale, West Palm Beach, and Sarasota. It was February, and the weather was not cooperating.

After bussing from Champaign to Chicago because their flight was cancelled, the band members hopped a plane to Washington. It is probably safe to say the nation's capital and its inhabitants don't react too well to snow, and the white stuff was falling heavily the day Medicare landed. What normally would have been a 15-minute ride from the airport to the hotel took an hour and a half.

Jim Vermette, who was the official Alumni Association representative on that trip, remembered getting separated from some members of the band who were riding in different cars. "We were literally going around in circles," he said. "It was a mess. I even think they started the concert without us."

Though the storm threw the band somewhat off schedule, they finally made it to the Botanical Gardens where they were slated to play. O'Connor remembered that, "It was a very pleasant setting, but musically it wasn't so great because it was in an all-glass building, and the acoustics weren't good. We sounded like a BB in a bath tub with the sound bouncing all over the place."

Perrino quipped that there were so many huge, green plants everywhere that they couldn't see the audience for the forest.

Next stop was Atlanta, and Murphy's law remained in effect. In the middle of a gig— the band was playing at a place called Aunt Mary's— someone from the Atlanta alumni club suggested to Perrino that he might want to announce to the audience that an ice storm was brewing outside. Such weather is taken very seriously in that part of the country, and it broke up the second part of the club's meeting and the performance.

"We were pretty casual about the whole thing since we experience a lot of that sort of thing—snow and ice—in our part of the country," mused Perrino. "So we just went back to the Holiday Inn in Peachtree Center where we were staying, had something to eat and went to sleep. When we woke up the next morning and looked out the window, lo and behold, there wasn't a soul in the downtown area of Atlanta. The precipitation was in the form of ice pellets, like BBs, and it was piled up about five or six inches high outside and nothing was moving." The big question was how were they going to get to Florida to honor their other commitments.

Vermette remembered making about a dozen phone calls and said, "Dan probably made a 100 calls to friends who might have private airplanes, to charter airlines that might be able to give us a lift out of there. We were calling all over the place— buses, cars."

Perrino told them the roads were blocked, and they were stuck. "After hours on the phone, I finally gave up and went to see what the other guys were doing. Stan had the largest room, and we used it as our headquarters. When I walked in, it was full of smoke—cigar smoke—you could've cut your way through it, it was so thick. A bunch of bored people were sitting around, lying on beds, watching TV. Ray Sasaki, who is Japanese-American and a member of the faculty who teaches classical and jazz trumpet, was on that trip. When I walked in and asked what was happening, they said they were watching old John Wayne war movies. And Sasaki pipes up, 'And I keep losing all the time.' That broke everybody up, relieving the tension."

Two days later, the band was finally able to get to the airport. They had to cancel their original flight plans because of the ice storm, and when they reached the airport there were people standing in lines everywhere. Perrino remembered, "We couldn't get a connection anywhere. I was in line at the Eastern counter, trying to find out how we could get out. I looked over to the next counter, Northwest, and the agent was by himself behind the counter and there were no customers. I jokingly said to him, 'You don't have any flights going to Sarasota or Tampa, do you?' It turned out he had one to Tampa."

By the time the group got to Tampa, it was late at night and they still needed to get to Sarasota. They ended up chartering a bus and arrived at their destination at 4 a.m., slept in that morning and were ready to play, at long last, for the fans in Florida.

&

In the early years, money conservation was always a big consideration. The band would make arrangements to stay with family members or friends when they played out of town. During that first Florida trip, friends of Morris and Frances Carter invited the couple to stay at their home.

Carter recalled that the distance between the friends' house and where he needed to meet the other band members presented a logistical problem. So the friend offered to drive him and his wife to a certain point on the interstate where they could join the others, who would be caravaning down the same road. A meeting time was arranged, the Carters were dropped off on the highway, and "We stood there for over an hour waiting for these guys to show up. It was a cold, cold day. Finally, here they came with Earle (Roberts) holding an Illini flag out the window. So much for trying to save money," he fumed.

The same flag would nearly flutter its last, however, on another leg of the trip. The caravan of cars was headed out of Miami a few days later, bound for Florida's west coast. Vermette was driving one car along what the musicians have since dubbed "Alligator Alley." Earle Roberts, who was sitting in the front seat next to Vermette, decided to open the window to get some air, and the flag fell out of the car. Carter recalled Vermette backing up the car and stopping to let Roberts pick up the flag. "He opened the door and saw a sign on one side of the road saying,

'Beware of Panthers,' and on the other side one saying, 'Beware of Alligators.' Jim said, 'Why don't we just leave the flag where it is and get out of here?,' but Earle gets out and picks it up anyway. Then Earle decided he had to go to the bathroom, so he went looking for panthers."

ॐ

As the "on the road" stories continued to unfold, it became clear that a sense of humor was as much a prerequisite for band members as was their musical talent. It seemed that when they least expected it, something would go awry, but the plucky members of the band would always rise to the occasion as they did on a trip to New York in the late '70s.

A dreary rain greeted the travelers as they stepped off the plane at La Guardia Airport. The infamous garbage haulers strike in Manhattan was in full swing, and the reeking stuff was piled high everywhere. Welcome to New York!

It was late at night, and the band was looking forward to getting out of the rain and to its hotel for a good night's sleep. They were booked into a place in the musician's district of the city, a hotel that Carter had suggested. "We should have known better," quipped Perrino, "because musicians are notoriously cheap. This hotel was terrible! The rooms were so small, we could barely stand up between the beds." Throwing economic caution to the wind, they made a unanimous decision to move to another hotel, a high-rise, the next day.

This one also presented a bit of a problem for O'Connor, but nothing the retired Air Force colonel couldn't handle. Being what Rahn calls "a fitness nut," O'Connor was used to taking a good run every morning. The congestion around the hotel presented a deterrent to this routine, but O'Connor, undaunted, made his morning runs anyway—up and down 12 floors of the hotel's fire escape, breathing in the aroma of rotting garbage rising from the street below.

The band was scheduled to give its performance for New York fans at an alumni club meeting at the top of the McGraw-Hill Building. The plan was to load up the van with musicians and instruments, drive the short distance to the building, unload, and take the freight elevator to the top floor.

For openers, the short ride ended up taking an hour and a half. The normal traffic congestion was bad enough, but the detritus of the garbage strike made it that much worse.

When they finally arrived at their destination, there was a fleet of trucks ahead of them, waiting in a long line to get into the basement of the building to unload their wares. The clock ticked away, and the band simply waited its turn in frustration.

"Finally," said Rahn, "it was our turn. It was like driving into the bowels of a cave. In this basement, there was a huge turnabout for these big semis to park because there was no room on the street, and it moves around until your slot gets to the loading dock. It was taking forever for us to get one of our slots on the turntable. By this time, our drummer, Bucky Wade, who was driving the van, got so exasperated by the whole scene that he decided to just park the van someplace else in the garage.

"One of these roustabouts yelled to him, 'Hey, you can't park there.' Well, Bucky let out a string of expletives, told him, 'the hell we can't,' and parked it anyway. As we grabbed our instruments and all strode by this guy, Bucky flipped him the bird."

A quick elevator ride bore the group up to the top floor and as they were starting to set up their equipment, "some young gal ran up to Dan and gave him a big hug. After his initial surprise, he recognized Mary Scott, a former student at the university, who had come for the concert. Turns out she was married to Bill Knack, who was editor of *The Daily Illini* the year before Roger Ebert," Rahn commented. For all the fuss and frustration, "We didn't have much of an audience," lamented Perrino. "It seems the bigger the cities we play in, the smaller the audiences."

In 1982, Medicare struck out on their second tour of California. No 24-hour marathons this time. They were back in the San Francisco area; it was Sunday, and a day to relax. Perrino recalls the group decided to take a little side trip to Muir Woods, a beautiful nature preserve of ancient, statuesque Sequoia trees and hiking trails.

"It was eight o'clock in the morning and I think we were probably the first people out there. It was a very misty morning and the sun was peeking through the trees. It was Stan's birthday, and his wife, Josie, Rudy James, and Harry Ruedi had also celebrated one that same month, so we decided to sing 'Happy

Birthday' to them. I'll never forget the magic of that moment. The acoustics in the woods made it seem like a worship service."

Later they elected to visit the wine country in nearby Napa Valley, but got sidetracked in Sonoma. They stopped and bought some cheese, salami, and sourdough bread, and had a picnic. "Then everybody just scattered—there were plenty of wineries to visit there, too," Perrino chuckled. "When they all came back, they were loaded down with at least 23 bottles of wine. I was tired and had stretched out on a picnic table. While I was sleeping, these guys lined up all these wine bottles around me, put a loaf of bread on my chest, and snapped a picture." Who says musicians don't have fun!

One of the longest tours the band has taken was a two-week excursion in 1989, when they entertained fans in Seattle and Portland, and on down the coast of California (including a performance for the Cal Tech student body at the behest of the university's president Tom Everhart, former U. of I. chancellor). The gremlin on this trip played a few tricks on Mo Carter, whom his fellow musicians claim is jinxed. Suffice it to say that on earlier trips, Carter had lost a horn in Los Angeles or had gotten to an airport only to discover his luggage was missing.

Carter's "luck" held out in Seattle, almost as if it were predestined. Perrino recalled getting ready to leave the hotel in Seattle for another leg of the journey. "This bus driver packed all of our gear, instruments, and luggage into the bus, and we started off in our usual caravan fashion, following the bus down the highway. All of a sudden, the doors of the luggage compartment on the bus popped open, and only one bag falls out. You wanna guess whose it was?" he laughed.

&

Over the 23 years of the band's existence, it has taken its road show out of state 16 times, including several trips to the west and east coasts, as well as Texas, Arizona, Missouri, and Wisconsin, the Liberty Bowl and the Rose Bowl. But, in the main, the band stays closer to home, entertaining thousands as it criss-crosses the state of Illinois, performing an average of 80 to 90 times a year.

Among the more frequent performances have been those given for alumni in Paris and Rockford, and their longest-running engagement—19 years—is an annual benefit to raise G.E.D. scholarships for high school dropouts, at Willowbrook High School in Villa Park.

April in Paris in 1980 took on a whole new meaning for folks in east-central Illinois. Medicare's first appearance in Paris rekindled memories of the best of jazz and swing from the '20s, '30s and '40s, helped launch an alumni club there, served as a jazz instrumentalist clinic for high school band members, a benefit for the band's alumni, and a reunion of some former Medicare members.

A reporter for the *Paris Beacon-News* reported, "The University of Illinois 'Medicares' rolled into Paris today, riding a floodcrest of notes from America's contribution to the musical world—Dixieland jazz.

"By mid-afternoon, more than 1,100 students had toe-tapped and clapped to the sound of authentic jazz and blues music ... banjo artist Stan Icenogle set the record for travel, arriving at his family home in Mattoon last night from his present home in Tyler, Texas, where he is an oil broker."

At the time, the audience in Paris was the largest the band had ever played for off campus. For the clinic, Perrino traced the development of jazz for the young students, from the mid-19th century, borrowing from marches, dance music, religious pieces, and African-American spirituals. In 1982 Medicare made its third appearance in Paris, and its popularity had only grown.

Similar receptions and crowds also have greeted the band in Rockford six times. Having performed jazz-gospel services in the Champaign area for years, Medicare was invited to do the same in 1983 at Rockford's First Presbyterian Church, a performance that was recorded and the second one that originated in the state's second-largest city.

The band also added to the warmth of a July day that year, playing on a cruise boat on the Rock River, and later returning to Sinnissippi Park along the river banks, where 2,000 people slapped their knees, clapped their hands, and danced to the hot jazz of Medicare, sponsored by the Rockford Park District and its director Webbs Norman, an alumnus, and the U. of I. Alumni Association.

❧

Road trips also require planning for places to eat, something the musicians claim they always do well. . . eat! Perrino is renowned for his ability to sniff out the best places to chow down.

"When we are in Chicago, Dan always thinks we ought to eat at Berghoff's," said Rahn. "I remember when we were playing on the Daley Plaza—a big, flat open area. We had three cars at the time, and when we got there, we asked where we were going to park. Dan just shrugged and said, 'Well, just pull up and park on the plaza.' So, we did, and then went to Berghoff's for dinner. When we came back, here are these two big, Irish, Chicago cops standing by their cars, waiting.

"Well, Dan usually leads the advance party because he's not that big or intimidating, and we came up and these cops asked, 'Are these your cars?' Dan said, 'Ya,' and with this air of innocence asked, 'Aren't we supposed to park here?' And the cop yelled, 'Get those damn things out of there right now.' He never even gave us any tickets," chortled Rahn.

In truth, it doesn't seem to matter where the band goes. After so many years, the good-natured personalities of the members have seen them through some pretty looney times, and their fame preceeds them, pulling crowds of enthusiastic listeners everywhere they perform. The good times, they just keep rollin'!

5

The Fans

"Grow the business" is a buzz phrase of the '90s in commercial parlance, and one strategy the Medicare band doesn't need to concern itself with. Its market share, in terms of its fans and the range of its audiences, has done nothing but grow in steady increments over the past 23 years, almost as if it had a life of its own.

What began in 1969 as a hastily put-together, unrehearsed performance by a bunch of almost-retirees in an attempt to ease campus tensions became a product that would appeal to all age groups, both sexes, and all races for generations to come. What corporate vice president of marketing wouldn't drool over such success? But the profit, for Medicare, is not charted in dollars and cents, but rather in friendships.

From young school children to the nursing home set, from service clubs to professional groups, from state fairs to a states governors' conference, Medicare has entertained them all. The band's appeal continues to warrant a seemingly endless array of invitations to play.

Audiences sense the camaraderie shared by the members of the band. Their friendship comes through with their interpretation of the music. Their style and warmth, their happy music-making, has made them exceptional ambassadors of good will and legends in their own time. They have played before more than one million people in nearly 2,000 performances, and their fans just keep asking for more.

To a great extent, the focus of the band's mission is as much education as it is entertainment. To a group of 200-plus fidgety grade school children, a lesson in jazz is an attention grabber. At Robeson Elementary School, on a cold January day in Champaign in 1992, the band came to play and teach.

Sitting on the gymnasium floor and arranged in rows from front to back—the youngest and smallest in the front, graduating in age and size to the back of the packed room—the children's attention was focused on the stage.

The lesson began with Medicare leader Perrino introducing himself and each member of the band. He asked each musician to give a demonstration of his instrument, from the ooompah of a trombone to the roll of the drums. A slide whistle drew laughter from the young crowd.

"Jazz is an American art form," Perrino explained, "born in New Orleans and developed by black Americans. In those days the music wasn't written down as it is today. It was something they might have heard being performed in churches or along the river front or on a ragtime piano, and they developed it into their own style of music.

"Work songs from the plantations developed into a style we call the blues. Ragtime is just another version of jazz gospel music. To play jazz," he said, "it has to come from the heart, and it is always improvised."

To wit, the band began to play a variety of tunes, drawing the children into the performance through song. As the concert moved along, little hands clapped almost involuntarily, broad smiles lit up the gym, and the students swayed rhythmically with the music. It ended with a chorus of "Way Down Yonder in New Orleans" capped off with thundering applause. Day's lesson completed. As Stan Rahn once said, "When we were young, there were all kinds of joints where we could sit in and learn Dixieland. But today, there is no way for the young to learn," except possibly through the goodness of Medicare.

Perrino added, "We feel that teaching our style of music to younger players (and audiences) is important. It is a part of our folk tradition, and we are trying to pass it on down."

Educating audiences in the fine art of jazz has been part of Medicare's program and reason for existence for years. In the early days, the band conducted mini-concerts and jazz clinics in and out of state. In 1978, a Paris, Illinois, newspaper reporter wrote that such events in the small town "packaged good music, good fun, and superb professional entertainment . . . rekindling memories of the best of jazz and swing from the '20s, '30s, and '40s for much of the audience, and introducing younger members into an era that is an important part of the musical heritage of America and the world."

One of the longest-running gigs for the band has been a 19-year pilgrimage to Willowbrook High School in the western suburbs of Chicago. It began in 1974 when Art Proteau, a member of the faculty with the U. of I. Extension Division and a band regular, became friends with Ken Smith, director of continuing education in the area. Smith was taken with the Medicare program and suggested that Proteau bring the band to the high school as a fund-raiser to help students who hadn't had the opportunity to finish high school to get their G.E.D.s and to go on to college.

The concept was a winner. As each year went by, the audiences grew proportionately. The annual concert has become a big event, and scholarship money has been provided to many students who otherwise might not have been able to make better lives for themselves. Eight hundred fans showed up for the 1992 concert, and among them sat 50 faithful who were present at the original performance in 1974.

At the second annual soundfest at Quincy College in 1980, the band played with the college jazz band and swing choir and were joined by a group of alumni who had some solid musical credentials of their own. Among them were Bill Herleman, president of Wurlitzer Organ and Piano Co.; jazz trombonist Bob Havens, a member of the Lawrence Welk Orchestra; and Sheila Flanagan, official organist for the Kansas City Royals. A standing-room-only audience cheered the performance.

The band also has provided demonstrations for music classes at the U. of I., at high schools around the state, for elementary schools and school bands, in performances at Wabash Valley College, Southeastern College, the University of Florida and at Cal Tech, to name but a few. Keeping the heritage of American jazz alive and well is as important to the group as making music and having fun.

In 1986, at the band's 16th anniversary concert in the Illini Union, the performance in the South Lounge prompted *Chicago*

Tribune reporter Jim Spenser to write, "A passing student removes his Walkman earphones and stops to listen. A young woman, riveted to her German text a few moments before, abandons her studies and begins to clap to the rhythm. All over the room grins overtake curious stares. Some of these people are happily familiar with what is going on. Others are pleasantly surprised. But no matter which camp they fall into . . . their body language speaks with a single voice: This is fun."

❧

University of Illinois alumni groups have, perhaps, been the staple in Medicare's long history. Around the state and around the country, the band keeps the alma mater fires burning in the hearts of the Illini faithful.

Testimonial letters reported by local media are not uncommon. A Springfield scribe wrote, "They have proved [to be] so popular that there would probably be an Illini uprising along the banks of the Sangamon (River) if they didn't appear."

A 1978 article in the Bloomington *Pantagraph* quoted alumnus and U. of I. trustee Robert Lenz, "The guys in the band have so much fun that it's infectious." Before the band started playing for alumni gatherings in the city, the local club had problems getting 20 people together for a meeting. "Now the crowds get bigger every year."

In 1984, after numerous appearances in Rockford, alumnus Randy Lindstrom could no longer contain his enthusiasm for the band. In a letter to the editor of the Champaign-Urbana *News Gazette*, Lindstrom spoke his mind.

"The past weekend, Medicare made its sixth (or is it seventh?) appearance in Rockford. Over the past few years, they've had a wide range of 'gigs' here, largely due to the cooperation and initiative of our Rockford Park District. They've played in a park band shell, at a 96-year-old synagogue-turned night club, on a riverboat, at a fashion show, for a high school workshop, and at the First Presbyterian Church. Last fall, they played a warm-up to a special Rockford appearance by Dr. Robert H. Schuller, pastor of the Crystal Cathedral in Garden Grove, California. The world-renowned evangelist promptly asked if some Sunday the group would perform for his assembled congregation of 3,000 and television audience of 3,000,000. Arrangements are pending.

"The good will that Medicare has promoted between our communities and with the university is immeasurable. We enjoy staying in touch with you through these musical ambassadors you send to visit us each year. Actually, we're envious of you folks in Champaign-Urbana. We wish Medicare 7, 8 or 9 could perform for us as often as they do for you. We know they can't and, perhaps, that's why each visit is so special to us. SRO crowds and standing ovations are the norm at each performance ... even in church." In fact, Medicare's fourth record album, all gospel music, was recorded live at Rockford's First Presbyterian Church in June 1983.

But all fans aren't dyed-in-the-wool orange and blue Illini. The band has touched thousands of people who, although unconnected to the university, embrace it with enthusiasm and loyalty. Eugene Rosen of Florrisant, Missouri, is one of them. And he has never seen the band in person.

In a letter to Dan Perrino dated Jan. 24, 1992, (the two have corresponded for several years but have never met face to face), Rosen wrote, "While I write this note, I am thoroughly enjoying listening to your second LP recording of Medicare jazz. I am certain you will recall how we became acquainted. I had found one of your records at my local library and bought it for 25 cents, fell in love with the music and then wrote to music stores in Champaign-Urbana. My name was passed on to you and a friendship developed.

"Well, about a month ago, I received a postcard from Old Main Bookstore in Urbana, telling me that they had an almost-mint-condition album of Medicare jazz and offered it to me for $6. My check flew to them and now I am the proud owner of this album (too)."

What's in a name? A postcard arrived in the Alumni Association's mailbag one day in October 1992 from a fan in Madison, Wisconsin, who wasn't quite sure what to call the band, but he sure knew what he wanted. "Please send us one of each of the cassettes of the cardiac and geriatric jazz group—one was a concert and one was not. We lost the order form. I'm enclosing a check for $22 to cover costs and shipping."

A woman from Glenview wrote a letter to the editor of a trade newspaper exclaiming, "I was given a two-record album of a great group of musicians from the Champaign, Ill., area, mostly present and former faculty from the University of Illinois. They call themselves Medicare 7, 8 or 9. Practically all of the Dixieland classics are included and each number is beautifully played and recorded. They claim they don't rehearse. I'm sure other jazz lovers would like to hear the album and watch for their concerts. Most numbers have a different group performing, each accomplished, all are real treats."

Audiences have been as varied as thousands of brown-baggers who showed up for noon-time concerts for eight consecutive summers at Chicago's First National Bank Plaza in the Loop, to concerts in parks on summer days. From conferences for grain dealers to performances with symphony orchestras. From small, private riverboat parties to dance marathons on the U. of I. campus. For small children, for residents at nursing homes. Even at funerals. And the first was at the invitation of the wife of the dying man.

Dan Perrino related the story. Ed Thompson, a retired oral surgeon, had been, at one time, a professional musician who played in the St. Louis area, had moved to Champaign-Urbana, and with the encouragement of his good friend and Medicare member Morris Carter, had sat in a few times with the band.

Perrino received a telephone call from Mrs. Thompson one day. "The phone rang," he said, "and it was Thompson's wife, and she said, 'You know Ed's not been doing too well and isn't gonna make it.' Now we all knew that Ed had cancer, but thought, up till that time, that he was doing pretty well.

"It was just before Christmas and I was on my way to the International Band and Orchestra conference in Chicago, where I was to be part of a panel and had been preparing comments for it and running behind schedule as usual. Then the phone rang and there was this calm conversation about somebody who wasn't going to be around much longer. Mrs. Thompson said Ed had been trying to give her some suggestions about a memorial service he would like and thought it would be good to have some jazz played, making it more jovial rather than somber. He wanted Medicare to play.

"She asked me if we would do it. Now whenever I get calls inviting us to play, I have to think about what it is, when it is, what the conflicts are, who is available, etc. Now we had never been asked to play at a funeral or a memorial service before, and my brain was rolling like a slot machine trying to think way ahead. When you have a funeral, you don't have weeks to plan something and I inadvertently blurted out, 'Well, when do you think this might be?' and as soon as I said it, I knew I had said the wrong thing. But she started to chuckle, and it made me feel a little bit better."

Medicare did play for Dr. Thompson's service, and Mo Carter remembered that afterward the funeral director came up to them and asked if they were available to do it again on a regular basis. They have since played for nearly 50 such services and at regular church services—Methodist, Lutheran, Baptist, Catholic, and Presbyterian.

ै

In the early '80s when Morton Weir was director at Boys Town in Omaha, Nebraska, he wrote of Medicare, "When I was vice chancellor for academic affairs (at the U. of I.) . . . I never tired of Medicare because they genuinely enjoyed making music. It was such a pleasure to observe them because the audience always knew that it was hearing people perform not out of a profit motive, but out of love."

U. of I. Alumni Association Urbana campus director Don Dodds reported less than 10 years after the band was formed, that "Medicare, without question, is the most effective program we have to offer . . . The enthusiasm the musicians generate is impressive. The response is always, 'Come back again next year.'"

Jim Vermette, former director of the Alumni Association, recently said, "I've been in churches with them, been in nightclubs, been in places where alumni have rented the space, seen them play with a piano that was almost falling apart, and seen them play in front of several thousand in Chicago. And they still play with as much vigor and enjoyment whether it's in front of 15 people or 15,000. They do their best all the time."

Back in 1977 during an interview with Joe Sutton, then-editor of the *Illinois Alumni News*, Perrino tried to explain why Medicare kept on playing.

He said, "We try to stay with the music current in the period from about 1900 through the '30s. It's classical jazz, or traditional jazz. For the man on the street, it's often 'Dixieland,' but that term is a colloquialism and actually has no meaning."

Try telling the fans that today! They know what jazz means; it means Medicare 7, 8 or 9. It means happy times are here again. Whether mini-concerts, jazz services in churches, performances with symphony orchestras, choirs or other bands, community performances at a Fourth of July parade or for senior citizens, for the Illinois Arts Council or a Cubs baseball game, the fans are there, clapping, singing, dancing—soaking up the good music.

6

Who, What, When, Where, Why

They make it seem so easy, so effortless, these Medicare people. In some respects it is, because they are such superb musicians. But don't let them fool you. Behind the carefree, fun-loving atmosphere, with notes flying through the air with the greatest of ease, every performance is carefully planned and orchestrated. Match play, so to speak.

Depending on the type of audience the band is scheduled to play for, when and where the performance will take place, and the nature of the request, leader Dan Perrino decides who will play, how many, and which tunes to select.

Perrino is the official organizer, coordinator, scheduler, recruiter, and logistics boss. His ear is never far from a telephone. In fact, pianist Donny Heitler once remarked in the presence of Perrino's wife, Marge, that he thought it would be a wonderful idea to buy "the boss" a telephone for his fishing boat, and Marge shot back, "Over my dead body!"

It's Perrino's job to intercept requests for Medicare performances, of which there are hundreds during the course of a year, and decide which to accept. These performances can range from informal mini-concerts for school children or nursing home residents to formal ones that are more demanding in an authentic jazz sense.

"It doesn't mean our performances will be any better or worse," he assures. "Hopefully, we always give our best. But we have to think in terms of who our audience is; what the listening repertoire is, and then match the musicians and tunes to that audience."

If a particular audience happens to consist of small children or senior citizens, the concerts are deliberately planned to be shorter in duration as are the tunes they will play because these groups tend to have shorter attention spans, Perrino explained.

"A more critical audience will listen more to the improvisation that takes place between the musicians—that means longer choruses and a longer program. It is important to know who the audience will be," and Perrino always takes this into consideration when planning a program.

In the Champaign-Urbana area, Perrino can draw on a list of 30-35 proven musicians. Once a date is inked in his little black book and he knows the type of audience, he deliberately selects those musicians and songs that he thinks will match that group of fans.

"When we have an older audience, we try to select tunes they are familiar with, whereas when we play to a more critical audience, our selections are more demanding in a jazz sense." With small children and other student audiences, the performances are linked to a short dissertation on the history of jazz and a show-and-play of the various instruments the band uses.

If the group is playing at a football tailgate gathering, they provide mainly background music, which is much easier to program. But if the concert is more formal, where people are sitting in an audience, the repertoire of tunes is chosen much more carefully. "We want to start out with a grabber—something infectious like 'Sweet Georgia Brown' or 'South Rampart Street Parade' and end with a good finish—usually 'When The Saints Go Marching In.' That's show business."

In between, there is always a variety of tunes that hold interest. And it is important that the audience is facing the band—"We always look at their faces," Perrino explains, using the audience's expressions as a barometer of how the musicians are doing. "We don't like to play in certain situations, such as when the lights are out, because we want to see the audience's emotions and smiles as we perform. It's a good way of measuring whether or not we are reaching them."

Once the date is made and the audience is known, then the musicians are selected on the basis of their playing experience. Perrino claims his own jazz-playing experience is more limited compared to Carl Johnson, John O'Connor, or Morgan

Powell. "They've done a lot more playing using improvisation, while my experience has mostly been with dance bands and reading the music constantly. My improvisation skills are not as good as some of the others."

Some musicians are more attuned to a certain style of music than others, simply because they've played that style more often. And others play more often, either several times a week, or take long engagements playing Dixieland. Still others may only play the Dixieland style when they sit in with Medicare. Perrino includes himself and Stan Rahn in that category.

"When we do full-blown concerts, I try to be sure that some of those people are in the ensemble so that we make sure the mix of experience ensures a good job," he said.

John O'Connor, said Perrino, is a master at mixing and matching musicians and tunes to audiences. Rotating personnel in the band is a strong point, he said. "It's the variety of players and different combinations that take place to serve certain functions" that's key, said O'Connor. "When Dan knows the nature of a certain event, he'll go after certain people—players that he knows will fit in."

Rotation of players is a deliberate act on Perrino's part. "For instance, we have four trumpet players in the area and each time we play, we begin by selecting one that hasn't played for a while, depending, of course, on their availability. That applies to all the instruments. There has to be a blending between the trumpet and trombone and the clarinet and saxophone. Each one has to be able to complement the other player.

"Everybody's part is important, and we have to be sure that everyone who is playing makes a contribution. The pianist, for example, is key, as is the rhythm section. Without the piano giving off the right chords or being able to accompany a singer, we're in trouble. We're fortunate to have some excellent pianists. Drummers are extremely important, too," he said, and the band is equally fortunate to have a number of very good ones from which to choose.

One trait that Medicare has that most other Dixieland groups do not, is its strong focus on vocalists. "We feel fortunate to have Stan (Rahn), Dena (Vermette), and Phyllis Denny, who has sung with the big bands, Barry Wagner, Harry Ruedi, who lends a vaudevillian Jolson style, and Rachel Lee," said Perrino.

"All of them are very fine singers, and we have found that one of the best ways to communicate with an audience is through the singers. While an audience likes to hear instrumental music, we try to balance a program with vocal as well, and that gives the variety we need to keep the audience's attention and also make them feel good.

"The voice is a great way to communicate, more so than instrumentally, unless it is an absolutely critical jazz audience. Then it's another ballgame. But a lot of audiences are not on that plane."

As for the selection of the music, while the band does play traditional Dixieland tunes, it also likes to play a wide range of jazz music. "Traditional jazz buffs would probably not play Duke Ellington," said Perrino. "We like to play jazz classics rather than Dixieland exclusively—somewhere in between. Most importantly, we want to reach the audience and entertain them. If we play over their head, we lose them.

"Our mission is different than a commercially oriented Dixieland group. That's how they get their jobs, and they must sustain themselves by those jobs. We don't have to worry about that because we just perform for alumni, faculty, students, etc., and most of our programs are on the shorter side."

Perrino, of course, is being overly modest. The band's audiences are much more far ranging than just the university community.

What really boggles the mind, especially for anyone who has ever heard Medicare play, is that all their performances are unrehearsed. That, again, is a testament to the quality and talent of the players. Improvisation is pretty basic with this group. That doesn't necessarily mean they never read sheet music or charts.

According to *Dixieland Dialogue*, published in the mid-'70s by the Continuing Education and Public Service in Music and the U. of I.'s Office of Campus Programs and Services, Medicare's "learning and performing differs from the conventional reading and playing procedure." This is accomplished "through the technique of transferring notated ideas into free form and re-recreated embellishments.

"When working up new arrangements or compositions, members discuss 'on the job' various musical thoughts which they have discovered from charts or by listening to live or recorded jazz performances. At this point in the creative process, individual and group experimentation begins—all improvised, nothing written. The ear becomes the focal point instead of the eye."

There is a family tree, of sorts, of jazz music, and many members of Medicare continue to explore various branches of that tree, whether it be the classical jazz that originated in New Orleans (ballads, religious songs, Creole chants, work songs, blues) or later styles in the mode of Louis Armstrong or Benny Goodman, Count Basie or Dizzy Gillespie.

The instrumentation of Medicare, *Dixieland Dialogue* reported, is patterned mainly after the classic New Orleans style of jazz—one trumpet, one trombone, one clarinet, a piano, tuba and banjo, plus Medicare's addition of a seventh instrument, the tenor sax. But over the years, there have been many variations in instrumentation, depending again on the type of performance and the audience. Substitutions are often made.

Outdoor performances require more differentiation in instrumentation than indoor ones. The big sounds of a tuba and banjo go over better outdoors, while a string bass works better indoors. Guitars can be substituted for banjos occasionally, cornets for trumpets, a sousaphone for a tuba. Two or more of the same instrument might be required in some cases, but always must complement each other. This is usually accomplished by trading solo choruses or "riff" patterns with other members of the band. And there is always room for additional instruments if the program requires it.

Getting it all together also requires the logistics of transporting band members and their assorted instruments from point A to point B. Many times, as in the case of big open areas such as parks and stadiums, or indoors in large concert halls, high-tech sound equipment is a necessity. Perrino makes the arrangements for all of that, too.

Sometimes, loading, strapping, and stuffing all of this humanity and gear into vans or whatever mode of transportation is used, and then trundling on down the streets and highways can evoke a scene right out of the Keystone Cops.

It ain't easy, but the end result is worth it.

Perrino insists that in the beginning "It was never our intention to form a group. We don't have any agenda or press kit;

we work purely on the basis of invitation. And the invitations are sometimes surprising, even to the small group. He has gotten calls from conductors of symphony orchestras as far away as Green Bay, Wisconsin, and Wheeling, West Virginia., wanting the band to appear with them.

While Perrino does his juggling act, Stan Rahn is kept busy as the band's accountant and business manager, another feat that isn't as easy as it sounds. Because the band is a not-for-profit organization, keeping records for the IRS and the musician's union, plus all the other extraneous expenses for travel, meals and miscellany, can be just as harrowing. John O'Connor takes charge of the educational aspects and arranges workshops and clinics.

After all is said and done, the enthusiasm and good will the band generates seems to be well worth their expenditure of time, talent, and energy. As Don Dodds once said, "The enthusiasm the musicians generate is impressive. The response is always 'Come back again next year.'"

7

The Boys and Girls in the Band

The numbers 7, 8 or 9 that follow the Medicare band's name originally referred to "however many showed up" for a given concert. In actuality, the gifted musicians who have tooted their horns, strummed string instruments, banged the drums and played the piano over the past 23 years number more than 100.

Sometimes a particular performance may only call for a few players, other times as many as 30, as in the case of an anniversary concert at the Krannert Center in the '80s. On special occasions, several different groups of seven or more musicians fan out in different directions in one day to accommodate all of the requests for their talents. This often occurs in the fall over busy football weekends when many colleges and departments at the university entertain alumni and friends homing in on the campus.

The caliber, as well as the number of musicians and vocalists who have played and sung with the band down through the years, speaks well for the organization. They are all top notch, or they wouldn't be invited to participate.

The talent pool Perrino draws from includes musicians of all sizes, shapes, and ages—both men and women. Many have been or still are leaders of their own jazz units or dance bands. Their professionalism lends leadership to the unrehearsed performances. And because they are pros, they are familiar with the selections to be performed and how a certain tune begins—four-bar piano introduction or "from the top." The rest is spontaneous, and the musicians make it work, creating the cohesiveness that makes the presentation work.

Warren Felts, a 70-something elder statesman with the group and a teacher of jazz, is a pro who cut his teeth on Dixieland right where it all began—in New Orleans. He has played bass tuba and string bass with the legendary Pete Fountain and floated down the Mississippi entertaining guests on the old-time Mississippi Queen and Delta Queen paddlewheel riverboats.

The student body has yielded some of the band's youngest members. Britta Langsjoen was a 20-year-old chemical engineering student in the late '80s when she played trombone with Medicare, the U. of I. Jazz Band, and other community ensembles. Her experience was so gratifying when she was with Medicare, that she decided to switch her allegiance from science to music. She left the chemical engineering laboratories behind and struck out for New York, where she is currently working as a nanny to make ends meet while she tries to break into the musical world of the Big Apple. Other student-members graduated and took their talents around the country. Many of them currently play in renowned musical groups and orchestras.

Even families have been involved, like the Helgesens. Gregg, a former jazz band leader and regular with Medicare, is a clinical psychologist at Carle Clinic in Urbana and an adjunct professor in the U. of I. College of Medicine. His son, Jeff, and daughter, Annie, can also call themselves Medicare alumni. Jeff is a professional musician who toured Europe with Ray Charles. Annie, like Langsjoen, was one of the youngest female musicians ever to perform with Medicare, and her sister, Cassie, has sung with the group.

Many others either have or continue to enjoy their musical careers in the "big band" spotlight. String bass virtuoso Jim Cox plays for Marian McPartland and has sat in with Earl "Fatha" Hines. Chuck Braugham, the original drummer with Medicare, is playing for Rosemary Clooney and Clark Terry. Other Medicare veterans, some who started playing as early as the 1930s, have performed with Les Elgart, Del Courtney, Orrin Tucker, Tiny Hill, Art Castle, Woody Herman, Dick Jurgens, Carmen Cavallero, Les Brown, and Stan Kenton. When the Jimmy Dorsey, Tommy Dorsey and Glenn Miller bands bring their entourages to the Midwest, they often call on Medicare musicians to join their ranks during regional performances.

They've played with symphony orchestras, for Steve Allen, Perry Como, Andy Williams, George Burns, the Ice Capades, and Ringling Bros. and Barnum and Bailey Circus.

Women have contributed significantly to the charm and appeal of the band, both as musicians and vocalists. Karen Korsemeyer, a string bass major in the university's School of Music, was the first female who played with the band. Jazz singer Phyllis Denny has performed with the Johnny Rinaldo Orchestra, a Stan Kenton-style group. Both she and Rachel Lee continue to add their considerable talents when called upon for Medicare performances.

Though most of the talent Perrino taps resides in and around the university community, some have moved to other areas of the country. But they are never forgotten. When the band is on the road, either traveling around the state or around the nation, Perrino consults his little black book of phone numbers and invites former Medicare players to grab their instruments and join in the area concerts.

The very heart of Medicare, however, still beats in a smaller core of musicians. They are either original members of the band or those who have played and sung on a regular basis down through the years. It is their stories, which follow, that bring the charisma and character of Medicare 7, 8 or 9 together.

STAN RAHN

Ma Goodwin, in her most strident Texas twang, simply yelled, "Forget it!" And Marshall Rip's little jazz band, contract or no contract, was summarily thrown out of her ramshackle roadhouse and left to its own devices somewhere in the Lone Star state.

It was the late 1930s, and Stan Rahn had been spending another of his summers between school terms in Minnesota, blowing jazz for yet another band. He had been persuaded to come to Texas to play with Rip's band by his older brother who lived in Corpus Christi.

"It was a wild summer," said Rahn. "It was a good jazz band, half of them Mexican college students. We went on the road and played all around Texas; even got so far as southern Illinois on that little tour."

But panic set in at Ma Goodwin's. She thought she had booked a country music band, "and after about the second night, she just said, 'Get out.' It wasn't her style of music." The group was living hand-to-mouth as it was, Rahn chuckled as he remembered the incident. "We had two cars and a trailer to drag all our stuff around in and only had enough money between us to send the cars back to Corpus Christi."

By the time they loaded the cars up, there wasn't enough room for all the band members, so Rahn and Rips hitchhiked nearly 500 miles through the heart of the state, making it back to home base in two-and-a-half days, sleeping in flophouses along the way. That experience was one of many that would eventually lead Rahn along the road to Illinois and to his charter membership in Medicare 7, 8 or 9.

"Steady as a rock," "smooth as silk," and the "glue that holds the band together" are terms used in describing Stan Rahn, a slim and trim six-footer who is still singing and swinging after all these years. Rahn is all of those things. . . and more. He is the perfect foil for the exuberance of a John O'Connor, the master showmanship of a Dan Perrino and the coquettishness of his most frequent singing partner, Dena Vermette. His is a quiet strength; tension is not a word in his vocabulary.

There is a genuine warmth that comes through when one talks to him and that his audiences sense when he sings—not jazz, but oldies and goodies, such as "You're Nobody Till Somebody Loves You." And does he love to sing!

Back in the early '30s, he was a first tenor in the famed St. Olaf (College) Choir, then under the direction of F. Malies Christiansen, at the time a world-renowned choral director from Norway. But that was merely a jumping-off point.

In the fall of 1992, Rahn got to reminiscing about his growing-up days in Buhl, Minnesota, a little mining town in the iron range north of Deluth. "Sounds like a soap opera," he laughed, as he started to recall how events in his past led to his musicianship and his eventual migration to Illinois after traveling around the United States and Canada in the name of music.

His mother was from Sweden; his father was from Denmark, and was a miner in Minnesota's north country. "Sometimes, things were kinda tough," he said, "but we had great winter activities," and in a town of about 1,200, there were always social functions going on between the churches and the local school.

He especially remembers the school because "with a small school like that (there were 30 in his graduating class), you had an opportunity to partake in everything. I was on the swim and track teams, and played clarinet in the school orchestra and band with my two brothers." It was also an excellent school academically, and the town had a great Carnegie library.

The reason for this prosperity was that when the mines were booming, all the mining towns would get a percentage for every ton of ore that was shipped out of the school district, Rahn explained. So the schools and the cities had lots of money, which made for good teachers.

After graduating from high school at age 16, Rahn attended a junior college in Hibbing. In those days, he said, any kid who went to either of the two community colleges (the other in Virginia)— both of which were 15 miles away— was paid $15 a month to attend. It was a good investment for the colleges, he said.

But after two years, Rahn was forced to drop out so his parents could send his older brother to the University of Minnesota. It was a fortunate move, because during the next two years he started playing saxaphone and was introduced to jazz through a small band in the area.

At about the same time, a woman from St. Olaf College had just joined the staff at the town library. She was a frustrated musician, said Rahn, and in no time had organized a little choral group that Rahn and some of his friends joined.

"She would stage these funny little concerts," he recalled, and apparently thought his singing talent deserved more attention. She talked him into enrolling in St. Olaf, which he did, and after two auditions he became a member of the college's famous choir.

Rahn's first contact with the U. of I. campus occurred on one of the many tours the choir would make, both at home and abroad. The choir put on a concert in Huff Gym and was put up at the plush Urbana-Lincoln Hotel. "All our tours were strictly first-class," he said. The 60 choir members traveled by train all over the Midwest and East Coast, singing in such showplaces as Orchestra Hall in Chicago. A special dining car was added on to the train just for the choir, and taxis would line up at the train stations, waiting to take them to the best hotels.

After receiving his bachelor's degree in social studies from St. Olaf in 1936, Rahn landed a job teaching in a little school in Wrenshall, Minnesota. He was paid $965 a year, but since jobs were hard to come by then, he was happy to be employed.

The following summer, the superintendent of schools thought Rahn needed to beef up his credit hours in physical education, one of the classes he had been teaching, so he headed to the University of Minnesota. It was during that summer that he met Snowball Johnson and his wife. "They played piano and drums . . . she had come out of the era of playing in the silent movies and knew all kinds of stuff," and he added his horn to the little group.

Three years later, Rahn had been made principal of the school in Wrenshall. But he continued to practice his music and had even joined the musician's union. As fate would have it, through a union newsletter, he spotted an advertisement for a tenor saxaphonist wanted by the Red Maxfield Band in Urbana. He answered the ad and by the following summer was playing with Maxfield, working at gigs all over southern Illinois, Indiana, and Michigan.

At the end of the season, one of the band members, Jack Kirkpatrick, persuaded Rahn to stay on with the band and go to graduate school at Illinois. Except for the 1942 school year, when he returned to Minnesota to serve as superintendent of the Wrenshall school district, Rahn had become a permanent resident of Illinois.

While he was earning his master's degree in public school administration at the U. of I., Rahn went on the road again. In 1940, a booking agent in Chicago who was a friend of a professor Rahn had been studying voice with was pulling together an octet to make the state fair circuit at summer's end.

He headed up to the Windy City for an audition and landed a job as a tenor with The Commanders, "a pretty elegant group," chuckled Rahn. "We had all kinds of fancy costumes and big opening numbers with 16 dancing girls." They hit fairs all over the country and got all the way up to Calgary in Canada for the big rodeo. He especially remembers seeing "that gal with all the feathers," Sally Rand, and her husband who was a world-renowned bronco-buster. "They had matching white deerskin outfits, a fancy trailer, and the whole shooting match," a real eye-opener for a young buck.

By 1943, Rahn was back in Urbana-Champaign, continuing his graduate studies and about to enter a new stage in his life.

"I was working for the housing division, which at the time was located in Illini Hall on Wright Street." It was during World War II, and most of the residence halls on the campus had been turned over to men. The second and third floors of Illini Hall became a dormitory for women.

"There was a lovely lounge on the first floor and a big grand piano, and many times during the noon hour, I would go in and play it."

One day, he spotted "a little coed. . . Leona Youngquist was her name, and she and my wife-to-be, Josie Grisham, were both living in that dorm. Leona went back and said to Josie, 'You've got to meet Atlas Maidenswoon,' that's what she called me," he laughed. Though Josie wasn't as taken with Rahn as her dormmate at first, the two were eventually married in 1947.

It wasn't long before the new bride put her foot down. Rahn had continued his involvement with bands around town—Bud Roderick and Dick Cisne. He did a lot of club dates—what Rahn called "bean jobs"—playing in small combos in the afternooon and at night at campus hangouts like Prehn's on Oregon, Prehn's on Green, and Hanley's. The musicians would be paid meal tickets worth about five bucks. But Josie didn't like being home alone so much of the time, so Rahn put his horn away and didn't pick it up again until 20 years later.

By 1969, Stan Rahn was executive director of the Dads Association, in charge of "500 student organizations," and working on Dan Perrino's staff. Being musicians, they knew of each other's talents, though they had never played together. That changed when Perrino made the telephone call during the student uprising in the Union . . . Rahn took his clarinet out of mothballs, rushed over to join the rag tag group, and history was made.

Though Rahn continues to play his clarinet with Medicare, he considers himself just an average player compared to the other musicians in the band. But he does claim a good ear, and can play well enough to fill in, he said. His real contribution is as a singer, and ballads are probably his favorite.

Rahn's humility tends to get in the way when others sing his praises. He merely shrugged when asked why his fellow musicians tend to regard him as the rock or the glue of the outfit. Maybe it's because he's the business manager for the band, he muses. Or maybe it's because at age 78, he's the senior citizen of the group. All he will say is that all his contemporaries envy him his hobby. And he loves every note, every song, every gig, and all his Medicare buddies. The beat just goes on, and when the call comes, he's still ready to answer.

JOHN O'CONNOR

It was 1943, and flight commander John A. O'Connor and his B-24 bomber group were heading back to base and safety after another harrowing mission designed to kick the teeth out of Hitler's war machine. The routine was the same. Each of the five crew members in O'Connor's plane, from bombadier to tail gunner, were poised in their assigned positions, band instruments in hand, awaiting the downbeat from the cockpit.

From the time he learned that several of his flight crew had band-playing experience, O'Connor's Irish impishness got the better of him. He suggested to the men that it would be fun, as well as therapeutic, to smuggle their band instruments aboard the bomber before takeoff and play on the way home to relieve the tension of the raid. The crew agreed, and mission after mission the commanding officer generously looked the other way as the little band in the air played on.

Music and the military are the two loves of John O'Connor's life—after Erma Jean, his wife of more than 50 years, and six children, two of whom are adopted and Korean.

Though a retired colonel in the U.S. Air Force, the 75-year-old O'Connor exudes the energy of someone half his age, bowls one over with his enthusiasm for life past and present, and is still flying a plane and blowing his horn with all the gusto of a rookie pilot and a hotshot bugle boy.

Much of his life is graphically and chronologically illustrated in two thick scrapbooks, each nearly a yard wide, which he keeps on a special shelf in his home in Champaign. Slender, wiry, and looking nearly as young as some of the photos in his albums, O'Connor is eager to show and tell about the intertwining of his musical and military lives as well as his connection and commitment to the Medicare band.

Born in Milwaukee, O'Connor started playing the trumpet after his mother bought him his first horn when he was in second grade. She was an accomplished pianist, acquainted with the likes of Irving Berlin, and was a big motivator musically in his young life, he said.

As he moved through all the basic music lessons in grade school and high school, he started playing with local jazz bands in Milwaukee and got hooked on loftier musical ambitions. He wanted to teach as well as play, and in 1939 he graduated from the University of Wisconsin-Milwaukee with a degree in music education, making his way through school by playing with some fairly renowned dance bands in Chicago—Eddy Howard, Del Courtney, and Stan Jacobson. He also had a sustaining engagement playing in a 10-piece band at Charlie Toy's oriental restaurant downtown in the Windy City.

After graduation in 1939, O'Connor moved to Shreveport, La. and began teaching. But with World War II in full swing, his stint in the classroom ended a few years later when Uncle Sam beckoned. Though never having been in a plane, he opted for the Army Air Corps, and thus began a military career that would span 47 years and take him all over the globe.

He flew on submarine patrol out of New Orleans for a year. "Not very many people know," he said, "that many American ships headed for the European and African theaters, were sunk by German submarines 100 miles out to sea from the mouth of the Mississippi."

He spent nearly two years flying heavy bombardment missions in Italy and Africa. Out of the 50 missions, he only lost two men. That was during one of three raids over the Ploesti oil fields, 30 miles north of Bucharest in Romania. The area was a Hitler stronghold and the Fuhrer's main source of oil for his war machine.

O'Connor recalled being the flight commander leading the formation the day the two men were lost. The resistance was fierce, and "We were very, very lucky to get home." For his efforts in bringing the rest of his crew back safely, he was awarded the Distinguished Flying Cross.

Business was business, said O'Connor, but there was always time for fun, and that meant music. His little band was mute at first because they had no instruments to play. But O'Connor took care of that during a routine supply pickup and delivery to Naples, Italy. During their stopover, he and the guys "bought Italian instruments for a song. We paid for them in cigarettes and food," he laughed.

After a little practice, "which was horrible in the beginning," the group got to be pretty good. Returning from their bombing runs, "We operated in our battle positions," he said. "Everyone had to stay in their spots, but we had intercom microphones" and could hear each other that way. "The downbeat would come from the cockpit . . . 'OK, guys, are we all ready to do "My Gal Sal?" All right, let's go.' We had a trombone, an Italian string bass, which was the hardest thing to hide in the airplane . . . we hid it in the bomb bay, and I'd play the trumpet with one hand and the other on the plane's controls. It was a mish-mash of noise, but a lot of fun."

Their group gained more than a little notoriety and soon formalized into a 14-piece band, recruiting players from other squadrons. With the blessing of the commander, who gave the group time to rehearse, they began putting on concerts. "We could even take our bomber and fly to the concerts," said O'Connor, "but that would dovetail with picking up or delivering equipment to wherever we were going."

The band not only played in little towns around the airbase and on the beaches for the local folks, but also for the Italian Consulate and the U.S. Navy brass.

In August 1944, O'Connor returned to U.S. soil, and after a little time spent recuperating from the shellshock of war, he was assigned to the officers communication school at Chanute Air Force Base in Rantoul. It was there that his University of Illinois connection commenced.

He remembered that all the time he was in Milwaukee, he wanted to go to the U. of I. for his master's degree because the school's band director, Dr. A. Austin Harding, was a good friend of one of his Wisconsin professors who had urged O'Connor to go and study under Harding.

Harding was more than pleased when O'Connor showed up on campus, since many of his students were still off fighting the war. He brought O'Connor into the music program, made him a member of the football band as well as his assistant (in the absence of his regular assistant, Mark Hindsley, who was off in Europe in charge of the Air Force bands).

But O'Connor was still attached to the military and eventually was reassigned to Mitchell Air Force Base in New York. When the war ended, O'Connor, his wife, and family headed back to Urbana, at Harding's invitation, and he enrolled as a graduate student.

After finishing his master's degree, and with help from Harding, O'Connor accepted a full-time position at the University of Puget Sound in Tacoma, Washington, where he spent four years as director of bands and the orchestra.

In 1950, at the outbreak of the Korean War, the government again beckoned O'Connor, who was in the reserves. Though working on his Ph.D. at the time, Uncle Sam gave him 10 days to report for duty.

For the next 15 years, O'Connor served his country in Korea, Japan, Germany, and the United States. During his time in Korea and Japan where he was an air traffic control supervisor, he managed to find time for his music. The Korean Navy sponsored concerts by the Seoul Philharmonic Orchestra, which O'Connor conducted.

He also found time for philanthropy, courtesy of the military. He was put in charge of opening an orphanage for Korean children in Seoul. The commander told him to round up the refugee kids who were hanging around the GIs by the hundreds begging for food. "We requisitioned a big, beautiful house . . . the former Japanese Embassy," said O'Connor, for the orphanage.

Five years later, after having been rotated back to the States, O'Connor was sent to Japan again. As part of his duties, he was required to check up on the orphanage he had established in Korea. As luck would have it, two of the children—a boy and a girl—who had taken his fancy earlier, were still there. "I said to my family, 'How would you like to adopt two kids?' and they all went for it," he recalled.

After turning down a command school opportunity in Biloxi, Mississippi, primarily because state law would not permit his Korean children to attend public schools, the O'Connor ended up back at Chanute. O'Connor said, "I never dreamed I'd be coming there again," and was delighted to renew his ties with the University.

He became good friends with Mark Hindsley, who had, by then, returned from Europe, and began playing first trumpet in the concert band. He joined the Marching Illini band as well, and often would literally jump out of his airplane at Chanute and drive like crazy just in time to catch rehearsals.

In the late '50s, O'Connor met Dan Perrino, who was then band leader at Urbana High School. Both musicians played in bands around Champaign and Urbana—O'Connor with Dick Cisne, and both with Johnny Bruce. The connection would bode well for the formation of Medicare, which was still a good 10 years away.

Eventually, O'Connor parted with the military after 24 years of active service. That parting had a lot to do with Perrino, who, by this time, was at the University and had sent O'Connor a telegram in the spring of '67 while he was stationed in Texas. The wire said a faculty position was opening up in the U. of I. School of Music, and would O'Connor be interested? He was.

So the O'Connor family finally rooted themselves in one spot. "It was just perfect," exclaimed O'Connor. "It was just the kind of job I was looking for. I was to be with the extension department organizing extramural courses around the state in music education and also handling activities in Urbana." Among the latter was the development of a Marching Illini band contest, which turned into a program called Superstate, the state high school band competition that has been held at the U. of I. every year since 1967. Under Perrino's direction, O'Connor also ran the University's summer music camp.

Before long, Perrino moved over from the Division of University Extension and the School of Music to the student services office, a move that nettled O'Connor somewhat, since he had specifically come to the U. of I. to work with his friend. Though they continued to play in various bands together, Perrino's participation began to wane because of job pressures, "and he pretty much put his horn away," O'Connor said.

That horn, and others belonging to the core of musicians who would become the Medicare band, came out of the closets that day in late November 1969 in an attempt to let the music of jazz "soothe the savage breast." The "Dialog in Dixieland Jazz" in the South Lounge of the Illini Union was an astounding success to musicians and audience alike.

"We played and blew our heads off," recalled O'Connor. "It was a real shocker . . . a bunch of old horn players right there in the middle of all that." And that, of course, was the beginning of a beautiful 23-year relationship.

Though O'Connor has been retired as associate professor of music for some years, his heart and soul are still in his music. And his head is often still in the clouds . . . still soaring in his flying machine, ready to land at a moment's notice and dash to campus, trumpet in hand, to join in another impromptu Medicare performance.

MORRIS "MO" CARTER

Morris (Mo) Carter's trombone was a mainstay on the Medicare circuit for years, and he still blows a pretty mean horn at age 76, though he does admit to having "lost his lip" for a while after a couple of bizarre accidents.

His penchant for golf caused the first one. He banged his head on a low tree branch while hunting down a hooked tee shot in his golf cart. "I guess I wasn't looking where I was going," he laughed. As a result, he suffered the first of two hematomas. The second one occurred after he fell asleep at the wheel late one night driving home. The car swerved off the road and smacked into a concrete embankment, demolishing the car. After several months of nursing his condition, Carter was back with his buddies in the Medicare band, seemingly no worse for wear.

That's just the kind of stuff Mo Carter is made of. The soft-spoken Kentuckian can be as brassy as the horns he has played over the years.

Unlike most in the original Medicare group, Carter was not born with a brass horn in his mouth. No one in his family had a musical background, and it wasn't until high school, when the band director was scouting recruits, that he picked up his first trombone. The sounds of music have intrigued him ever since.

He studied music education at Murray State University, where he met his wife, Frances, and taught instrumental music after graduation in the Cincinnati area. He played in a lot of show bands around the Queen City before being inducted into the Army in World War II. Even then, music was part of his life. He played with the 78th Infantry Division band, "a gorgeous outfit," he reminisced, when the troops weren't in the thick of battle.

Honorably discharged from the service in 1946, Carter was anxious to go back to school for further study. He arrived at Illinois by way of Northwestern University, where he had been admitted but couldn't start until June since all the classes were packed with GIs.

"That was in the days when the Illinois Central Railroad would run five or six trains back and forth, and one of my GI buddies was working on his master's at the U. of I., so I stopped between trains to see him. His name was Webb Hoel, who later directed the Men's Glee Club, and he wanted me to stay overnight. The next morning he took me to see a professor at the School of Music. I was very impressed and decided this was where I wanted to go to graduate school."

That little layover in Urbana-Champaign turned out to be a life-long stay. When Carter finished his master's degree, he was talked into staying on to teach a summer session; one thing led to another, and before he knew it, he was a member of the faculty.

Carter loved being in the classroom teaching theory, not performance, he said. Though he would become assistant director of the school, he always maintained his faculty rank because he wanted to continue to teach. After 38 years, he retired as professor emeritus.

During the intervening years, Carter, like so many others who would end up playing for Medicare, performed with local campus dance bands. Especially when he was in graduate school.

"I had to eat," he emphasized. "Nobody had any money, the place was loaded with GIs, and most everybody needed and wanted a part-time job."

The big band sound was very "in," and Carter played a variety of horns, tuba and trombone included, with Dick Cisne and Johnny Bruce all over central Illinois and many times in Chicago.

When the big bands broke up, Carter said, his horn-blowing days began to wane. He became so wrapped up in his duties at the School of Music that, "except for a jam session now and then, I didn't do much of any playing for 15 years."

He, too, got a call from Dan Perrino in November 1969. "Dan said he had talked to John and they were thinking of getting a Dixieland group together and going down to the Union and start playing at noon to try to settle the kids down.

"Those kids weren't even born when Dixieland music was popular . . . they didn't know anything about it. All they knew about were the Beatles and rock. They were enthralled with us. Lloyd Berry wanted to know if we would do it every Friday noon hour. I remember Dan telling him, 'Hey, Jack, we've got jobs—we gotta go back to work at 1 p.m.' Peltason was always a big supporter of ours."

Carter has a lot of memories after more than 20 years of playing with the band. As its reputation started to spread, so did the band's field of operation. One road trip out east started its swing in New York, then Baltimore, ending in Washington, D.C. Carter particularly remembers playing at the Smithsonian Institution at the invitation of Jim Weaver, an Illinois graduate and then curator of the music museum.

He also remembers one of the first funerals the band played at. "My close friend, Ed Thompson, who was an oral surgeon at Carle Clinic, died. In his younger days he was a jazz musician, and his wife, Betty, asked if we would please play at his memorial service. So we did, playing standard hymns in a classical New Orleans jazz style. The funeral director was so taken by our performance, he wanted to know if we were available to play for other services, and what did we charge."

One of his most frustrating experiences, he recalled, happened when the band went west to play for and join in the 1984 Rose Bowl festivities. A truck was supposed to meet the plane when it landed in Los Angeles, load all the band instruments and deliver them to the hotel where the group was staying.

"About midnight, I went down to the loading dock, and as the instruments were unloaded, I noticed mine and Dan's were missing. When I went to the hotel desk of the travel agent that was handling the Illinois group and told him about the missing horns, I got the royal fluff from him.

"I started to leave when a young woman, also associated with the agency, walked over and said she had overheard the conversation and would I like her to make a few phone calls to see what she could find out. About an hour later, she tracked down the instruments—they had been on the truck all along, which was now clear across the city unloading more luggage and stuff at another hotel where fans were staying." An agent at the other hotel called Carter, apologizing for the confusion, and offered to keep the instruments in her own hotel room overnight for safe-keeping. They were hand delivered to Carter and Perrino the next morning, and the band played on.

If anyone is going to lose something, Carter will. If some kind of accident is going to happen, Carter won't be far from it. He usually takes it all in stride, but there was one time when he had just had enough. He laughs about it now, since years have put distance between him and what he calls "that awful, terrible" last leg of a tour Medicare had taken to Arizona.

The band flew into St. Louis from the tour out west, landing about 5 p.m. at Lambert Field. They were all pretty bushed, but still had one more gig to play for a group of St. Louis alumni before heading home.

"Dick Cisne and I had driven a brand new Ford station wagon, a university loaner, to the airport before we left for the southwest, and parked it there," Carter began to relate.

"We played for this group of alumni and about 9:30 p.m., he and I picked up the car and started going out of town on Interstate 70. I remember it was a horrible, rainy night.

"All at once, we began to have car trouble—something with the electronic system. We knew we had to get off the highway, and I was looking for the first exit I could find. I saw one and just as we started to turn off, the whole system went out and we just coasted down the exit ramp. Luckily there was a truck stop at the bottom. These guys came over and pushed the car into a repair bay. By then it was 10:30 p.m., and not only were we beat, we were pretty frustrated.

"They called a mechanic who came out, and after looking the car over, he said he couldn't fix it. Well, we didn't know what to do. There was this little greasy spoon connected to the truck stop, so we just ambled over, went into this cafe and ordered eggs, toast and coffee. It was now some time in the wee hours of the morning, and we were both bleary-eyed from the long ordeal.

"The mechanic had told us we would have to have the car towed to Collinsville the next day for repairs. Dick and I were sitting there, eating, both of us mad as hell. A guy in the next booth had overheard us talking about our troubles and walked over to our table. He said his rig was headed for Indianapolis and could take us as far as Effingham, so Dick called his wife, Lil, and told her what was happening and asked her to meet us in Effingham about 6:30 a.m.

"In the meantime, another guy, who was working behind the counter, came over to our table and said he felt bad about the trouble we were having. He said he could put the two of us up for the rest of the night in a room upstairs where a lot of the truckers stayed from time to time. He said it wasn't fancy, just a few cots, but we were welcome to use it. 'Course, Dick had been really fuming this whole time and when this guy made his pitch, Dick really erupted.

"I'm not gonna stay in some place where they carry on with these women they (truckers) bring in with them . . . we'd probably pick up some kind of disease."

So instead, the two got in the big 18-wheeler headed for Effingham. "We sat three across in the cab, our horns stuffed in the back," Carter recalled. "The driver was a tobacco chewer and had this coffee can hanging on the inside of his window by a wire. All the way to Effingham, he kept spitting in that can. Dick kept scooching over nearer to me as the trip wore on. We finally made it to Effingham where Lil picked us up and we thankfully headed for home."

Despite the occasional black clouds hovering over him, Carter takes it all in stride. After all his years with the band, he isn't about to pack it in. When the phone rings and Perrino has another gig lined up, he'll be there—if he can find his horn!

DONNY HEITLER

When Donny Heitler's hands caress the piano keyboard, ears perk up and listeners take note. Like his friend and mentor, the legendary George Shearing, it doesn't matter if he can't see what he's playing; Heitler feels it in his soul and his music takes on a life of its own.

Like Shearing "I was born blind, but I don't think of it as a handicap," he waxed philosophically. "It's just a nuisance." When he was 11 years old, a doctor operated on Heitler's eyes, giving him a tiny window of light in which to view the world. "It helped me to see a little bit, but you wouldn't want to see me drive down Green Street," he chuckled.

Part philosopher, humorist, and gifted musician, Heitler has had a life-long love affair with music, and his audiences over the years, including those with Medicare, have felt the passion.

At 50-something, Heitler doesn't quite fit into the age bracket of the so-called "old guard" Medicare regulars, but he's earned his stripes time and again, traveling across Illinois and the country entertaining the faithful. And unlike many of his cohorts who are engaged in other careers and professions, making music is his full-time gig.

Heitler has been playing in one band or another since he was in high school, but his interest in music began as a child in Pekin, where he remembers picking out tunes he heard on the radio on an old piano. He didn't take it seriously, however, until he was enrolled in the School for the Blind in Jacksonville.

"They had a marvelous music department at that school," he recalled over a martini at Timpone's restaurant in Urbana. "I was in second grade and my first teacher, George Gerlach, taught me to read braille music." The lessons were meant to be serious, but Heitler was really more interested in popular music and improvisation. "As often as not, when I was supposed to be doing my lessons, I'd be diverting my attention to tunes I'd heard on the radio or trying to explore the geography of the piano."

"I remember my first classical piece, 'Violet,' and then went on to other pieces. When Mr. Gerlach left, Edward Jacobs became my teacher, and I started studying Beethoven and Mozart, but I'd still jam in the evenings."

His real mentor in music, Heitler contends, was a novelty shop owner in Jacksonville, Boots Brennan, "a real keyboard player." "Back in those days, all the kids would go down to Boots' shop, which had an extensive record department, and we'd listen to all the newest recordings in these little booths. One day, Boots said to me, 'Donny, I want you to come in the booth and hear this blind piano player. It'll scare you to death. His name is George Shearing.'

"I was about 10 years old at the time, and I listened to George playing 'I Only Have Eyes For You,' something I've played since time and again over the years. Boots was terrific to me. He'd say, 'Why don't you take that home and listen to it for a while, then you can bring it back in a week or so.'

"One of the kids at school had a big record collection, and I'd go into his room and ask him to play his Nat King Cole records for me. That's how I learned all that stuff—more out of the classroom than in one."

But Heitler does credit both of his School for the Blind teachers for encouraging his talent, though he recalls that it was easier and more fun to improvise on the popular pieces than concentrate on the rigors of classical discipline.

It was Jacobs who finally laid down the facts of musical life. "It was when I was in high school, and I went in for a lesson with Mr. Jacobs. I could sense something was in the air. He said, 'We have to have a little talk, Don.' And I thought, 'Oh, oh.' He told me that if I didn't really work on the classics that I would never really gain what I wanted out of music. He said, 'There's no doubt you could play in the Hotel Baltimore right now, but you gotta trust me. You gotta do it. If you don't, I can't work with you. It's wasting your time and mine.'"

Two years later, Heitler played the first movement of the Schuman piano concerto at graduation, and Jacobs came over to him and said, "Do you remember that day when you were a sophomore and I called you into my office? That was the hardest day I ever had as a teacher." Heitler remembers telling him, "It was tough for me, too, trust me."

In his reverie, Heitler says it's that teacher he has to thank for keeping him on the right track musically. In fact, Jacobs treated him much like a son.

"I remember he took me to Chicago to hear my first name act. It was Duke Ellington, and he was playing at the old Blue Note in the basement at Madison and Dearborn. I'll never forget it. Afterward, we went to a place called The Streamliner where Don Shirley and some others I used to listen to on WENR radio in the evening were playing."

His earliest experiences at playing in bands were as a high schooler in Jacksonville. There was one local quartet in particular—"We would do gigs on Friday and Saturday nights at The

Hub at McMurray College. That was in 1953. I earned $14 a week. Can you believe it? That was a lot of money then. I mean, a malt only cost 15 cents. My meals and room were provided at school, so I really didn't have any expenses. It was wonderful. The night watchman at the school would let me in after hours. I had special permission to stay out later for these gigs."

The importance of his schooling in Jacksonville made a deep impression on the pianist. He not only learned music in braille, but his regular studies as well. He said he received prep training for college when he was a junior through the local high school. "That was to interrelate with the sighted world and as such, it (the school for the blind) was really a forerunner of the mainstream."

After a short stint at Illinois Wesleyan, where he continued to study music, he transferred to the University of Illinois at the urging of friends. He continued an active career in playing piano while he got two degrees in music and one in guidance counseling.

After receiving his first degree, the call of the open road beckoned. "I had a job waiting for me," he said, "and I went out for about a month, but then began to think I should go back and get my degree in education, knowing it wouldn't be easier to do as I got older."

"There was a yearning to stay on the road, but there is always something you learn around a college or university," and he learned a lot about life from both, he said.

"The thing that came easiest to me was playing standard tunes and improvising on them. I love jazz and picked up easily on that, too. I never wanted to be, nor could I have ever been, anything within shouting distance of a concert piano player. I didn't have the technical wizardry, the drive, the photographic memory (something his fellow musicians would vehemently deny), the composite that it takes to be that.

"But I did have things that enabled me to be a competitive person in the music marketplace in the areas in which I was interested and in which I continued to grow."

&

The comparison between Heitler's style of play and that of the great George Shearing is immediately apparent to audiophiles of a few generations past. And perhaps it was not only Shearing's style of play that so entranced a young Heitler, but also the blindness they shared. In any case, fate eventually brought the two of them together.

It happened in 1956. Heitler was a freshman at Wesleyan and a friend of his asked him to help his sister who was a vocalist, by playing for her audition for Mercury Records in Chicago. The sister's name was Peggy O'Neil. Heitler, being a good friend, agreed. After the audition, Peggy mentioned that both Teddy Wilson and Shearing were playing in town, and she wanted to repay Heitler by taking him out to hear one of them. He opted for Shearing.

The event is as clear in Heitler's mind as though it were yesterday. "It was a Thursday night. George was playing at the new Blue Note, and there weren't very many people in the club that night. After a couple of sets, Shearing left the stage and his guitar player, Toots Tielman, sat down at a table near us. We got to talking, and pretty soon Toots asked if we would like to meet George."

The meeting took place, and in Heitler's words, "We became instant friends." In fact, this idol of the young pianist invited him and his friends back to his hotel room that night where he continued to play just for them. "I remember he said he has just signed a deal with Capitol Records—it was that first album he did with strings containing 'September Song' and 'Autumn Leaves.'"

Some time later, Heitler got up enough nerve to call Shearing and ask him if he wanted to go to a Walter Geesigen concert in Chicago. "George said, 'If you can get tickets, we'll do it; and come on up and let's have dinner.'"

The friendship blossomed, but Heitler was always reticent to play in Shearing's presence. "I remember we had a little trio here in Champaign-Urbana, and I asked him if he might listen to us audition for him. But I ended up cancelling it because I just didn't think we were ready to play for him."

Some years later, Heitler did play for Shearing. "I was living and working in New York, and George would come to my apartment for a visit. He learned more about my playing then.

But you can imagine how hard it is to play for a person with that sort of . . . ," Heitler's voice trailed off. "I mean, he's George Shearing. What can I tell ya?"

It was because of their friendship that Shearing was part of a performance in the Illini Union in the 1970s that Perrino put together. Shearing returned to the university community a few other times to play, once with Mel Torme.

"I like the chords that Shearing uses," said Heitler. "A lot of what I've grown to do today can be traced back to what he taught me on his recordings and in person. That's always the kind of thing I wanted to do in music."

Over his career, Heitler has played with some of the best—Dick Hyman, who got jobs for the pianist in New York, Grady Tate, Jay Lenhart, and Urbie Green.

In fact it was when Heitler was living in New York that Medicare first got started. "I never even knew about the famous Medicare day. I had met Danny (Perrino) when I was in school at the U. of I. We both played with Johnny Bruce's band along with a lot of other faculty members.

"I look back on those days—those jackets and bow ties we wore and the trips we used to make—we had great times together on that band. I knew Dan was a wonderful person, but I didn't know him singularly above other members of the band at that time.

"I always loved Danny; he was the same Danny then that he is today. I didn't know that he was that deep or as broad in his human interest and human activities because we just played in the band together."

But that all changed in the fall of 1973 when Heitler returned to the Champaign area. "Danny asked if I would like to play a little Dixie with this little band and that's how I got started playing with Medicare. I've enjoyed so many performances with them, working with the Alumni Association and playing before all kinds of groups. I can't tell you how much I have enjoyed and appreciated the trips that we've taken. They are educational as well as social, and I'll treasure them forever.

"In totality, Medicare is a singular experience for me in terms of representing more than music. When you become personally involved and related to people that make music together, it becomes very special.

"I mean, are we talking about music here or are we talking about humanity? Medicare is really a family. I may have had experiences of working with George or Urbie Green or Dick Hyman, and Medicare has some very fine musicians, too . . . but they're like family to me. And the unique thing and the reason for that is Dan.

"If I could have every day as good as my Medicare days, I would have a very, very good life."

&

Heitler's piano accompaniment for singers in the band employs probably his greatest skill, he says. "You really have to listen to the music, and the reason I like to accompany really good singers is because I know what they go through to get where they are. You know, you gotta pay your dues if you're gonna sing the blues," he waxes.

"Some of them have sung in dives and honky tonks in front of unappreciative audiences. Sometimes that adds to their musical experience. We all take our lumps in this business. Heck, I just figure I'm singing through my fingers and a trombone player is singing through his horn, but a singer gets real close to you . . . like we're talking, not singing. He or she has the luxury of the lyrics and the melody. If they know how to deliver the lyrics, then it's a lot of fun to play for them."

These days Heitler keeps very busy playing not only with Medicare but at any number of places around east-central Illinois and occasionally in Chicago. He is also in the business of publishing piano arrangements of standard tunes, working closely with Jim Lyke at the university's School of Music.

"Jim had me do a couple of arrangements of old Irving Berlin tunes and took them to a keyboard editor who works for a division of Columbia Pictures, and she loved them."

The keyboard maestro is also contemplating recording his music for the first time on cassette. He confessed he could have sold a bunch after a recent performance, "But I'm the world's greatest procrastinator," he laughs.

There are some who won't let him procrastinate for long, however, including Mr. Medicare himself, Dan Perrino. After all, with a talent like Heitler's, akin to that of his boyhood idol George Shearing, the world deserves to hear his sensitive intepretations of some of America's best-loved pop standards.

DENA VERMETTE

Moody blues, ballads, and jazz—Dena Vermette has sung them all. But above all, this 5-foot-4ish, curvaceous brunette with a Type A personality, flashing brown eyes, and melodious voice confesses that Gershwin's "Someone To Watch Over Me" is her all-time favorite. The classics in the pop music category send her. And when she sings them, she sends her audiences too—into a warm reverie.

Dena's love of music and of singing goes back to her high school days at Ursuline Academy in Springfield, Illinois, an all-girls' Catholic High School "where I started studying music— classical and opera—with an incredible teacher, Carlton Eldridge, who was blind and wonderful," she reminisced on a warm summer day in 1992.

"He knew from the beginning that my heart wasn't in that kind of music because I would go home with an assignment and instead of singing it the way it was written, I'd want to improvise."

Dena Petrelli Vermette's Italian heritage may be partly responsible for her little stubborn streak as well as her outgoing, warm personality and singing talent. In any case, all of the above were showcased at a school talent show in 1957 when she surreptitiously replaced a tune she was supposed to sing with her favorite, "Someone To Watch Over Me."

"The first row (in the audience) was all lined up with the priests and nuns, and one of the qualifications to enter the contest," she snickered, "was that it had to be a classical tune. I looked over the repertoire that was handed to me and I thought, 'oooph,' it just wasn't for me. I got together with my accompanist and laid low until the last minute . . . I didn't tell her what I was going to do." But Dena's instructor got wind of the change and asked her, "'Dena, what is this?,' meaning it wasn't classical enough," she said. "And, I said, 'It'll be okay . . . just trust me.' So, I sang it and I won. Afterward, I remember someone saying to me, 'You know, one of the priests in the front row had tears in his eyes.' It's just that kind of song—that's why I love it because the words are so beautiful; it's just timeless. People loved that song then, and they still do today."

After studying music and elementary education at college in Florida, Dena began singing in her father's Springfield restaurant, The Black Angus. "We had an every-Friday-night jazz thing. I sung a lot of tunes like 'Misty' from that era, and we would pack 'em in. Sometimes it was Dixieland. I remember we had a trio, kind of like Medicare, in that whoever was available and could play would show up, and I would sing. Then, after about a year, it became a piano bar, and I would just stop in some evenings and sing for the fun of it. And that's where I got a lot of the training I am using now. The cabaret is the best experience in the world—to sit on a stool and take requests."

It was during the '60s, while working in her dad's "cabaret," that Dena's destiny as a Medicare singer began, though she surely didn't know it at the time. A young, Air Force National Guard reservist, Jim Vermette, spent many weekends in Springfield on duty away from his regular job as field director for the University of Illinois Alumni Association. He frequented the Petrellis' restaurant, not knowing at the time that the beautiful young woman with the sultry voice who sang there would eventually become his wife.

A mutual friend, whom Dena knew from high school and Vermette was stationed with in the National Guard, introduced them. Dena remembered Jim saying after the two of them met for the first time, "You know, I saw you in your dad's place when I was there for dinner sometimes."

The couple started dating that summer and were married the following April. Vermette went on to become the youngest-ever executive director of the Alumni Association, and as far as Dena is concerned, "I probably would not have had a chance to do much singing (after their marriage) if Jim had not been connected to the Alumni Association."

"I was meeting Jim for lunch at the Illini Union one day, and afterward we ran into Dan Perrino in the hallway just after Medicare had finished giving one of their performances. Jim stopped Dan to ask him how everything was going, introducing me in the process, and Dan replied, 'Great! Just finished a concert.' That's when Jim told him, 'Well, Dena sings, would you be interested in hearing her?'

She started singing with Medicare the very first year of its existence, as many as three or four times a week because the group was in such demand. For a while, she was the band's only female vocalist, performing at student residence halls, fraternities, sororities, constituent groups on campus, and in front of alumni groups.

Of her many performances through the years, a few stand out among the rest, particularly the big Quad Day concert in the spring of 1970, which she described as being "like a huge variety show" in front of thousands of people. There was a lot of talent involved at the time, she recalled. "Dan was kinda testing the waters right then to see who would fit in with the band."

There was many a Dads Day night at the old Thunderbird in Urbana, when students would bring their fathers, who were on campus for the traditional parent/son/daughter weekend, over to hear Medicare play. Often as not, paternal veterans of prior Dads Days would bring their own musical instruments, and Perrino would invite them to sit in and play. "We really packed them in in those days," Dena said.

There were many road trips over the years, crisscrossing the state to a variety of alumni gatherings, and others as far away as New York, Florida, and Arizona. The crowds were always enthusiastic and appreciative, and yet one gig that sticks in her mind is one the band performed in Chicago for a couple of years.

"We used to perform during the noon hour outside the First National Bank building in the Loop. People would come with their brown-bag lunches and sit and listen. It was always packed, and it was such a neat feeling." Those concerts were eventually discontinued, however, when the local musician's union put a stop to the non-union bunch from downstate.

Like all the other Medicare veterans, Dena has a fond feeling for the band's leader. "Danny's very fatherly toward all of us. On an actual gig, when we are on stage, he will be giving me instructions while I'm singing," she says. "He'll lean into my ear and say, 'Now, Dena, after you finish the first chorus, take another full chorus and then introduce Mo and have him do a half and then you come back in and take a three out of the bridge.'" When asked how in heaven's name she can keep track of what she's singing while all these good-intentioned instructions are being whispered in her ear, she laughs.

"Sometimes I don't. Sometimes I completely lose track of the words, but I never stop. I learned that long ago . . . you never stop. You skat or do whatever you have to do. So, if I forget the words, they may not make a bit of sense to the audience, but I'll just make them up and keep going.

"A few times he (Perrino) has really nailed me, though, and I'll have to stop, but that's just the way he does things, and there's no formality."

The informality of the group also spills over into planning what songs are to be sung. "Danny will have a list of tunes ahead of time that he knows I know and that he likes. Sometimes we'll argue over one, but 10 years later, a song I thought was corny in the beginning, I'll really end up liking. More times than not, he will call and say, 'Now Dena, for tomorrow's concert, would you consider blah, blah, blah. Now, do you have the key?' And, I'll say I'm not sure, so he'll run down to his basement . . . ping!, I can hear him hit the note (on the piano), then he'll say, 'Does that sound right? OK, sing some of that for me.' So that's how we rehearse, honest to God. And then later, he just brings this little list with the key to the concert."

Perhaps there's a little deeper understanding between the two "Ds" (Dena and Dan) because of their Italian backgrounds. Dena related one story, in particular, where it came into play.

"We were playing at this big hotel in Springfield and there was this trombone player, an alumnus of the U. of I., who found out Medicare was going to be in town and wanted to play with us. Now, I had known this person before, and he was a real ham, but Danny is always gracious and invited him to play. The trouble was, we couldn't get rid of him.

"Normally, a person will play one or two tunes with us and then sit down. But when this happened, it was the first time I noticed Dan's Italian heritage coming out . . . he would do this 'Na-na-na-nahhh,' kinda under his breath, when this guy would try to play more, which means, Italian-style, 'Please leave!' Sometimes he'll do it with me too. When we're talking about my singing a certain tune, he'll say, 'Well, Dena, I think . . . na-na-na-nahhh . . . I don't think.' You know, that kind of thing. He knows how to graciously get rid of pests along the way."

Some of her fondest memories of Perrino are almost motherly. "A funny bit about Dan," she said, "is he is always falling asleep in the corner of airports. There he is, this little, rolled-up bundle just snoring away, cuz he doesn't sleep very well at night.

"Dan makes everyone feel like family," she says, and the other members of the group are like brothers and sisters. Earle Roberts "is Mr. Positive. The first thing he'll say to me is, 'I'm right, honey.' In other words, all is well with the world and with him. He always milks the audiences. He is a real professional and a gentleman. He always comes prepared with jokes to tell. He carries around this little book. The naughty, off-color jokes, he'll tell to the fellas, but he'll call me aside and whisper, 'Sweetie, I brought my Dena book.' He has separate, clean jokes just for me. Isn't that cute? He's a real character."

On John O'Connor, Dena relates, "He always gives 110-20-30 percent every concert. He just wouldn't know how *not* to do that, and it is infectious. When he plays, I tend to give it a little more because when he's there I feel confident, and I know the concert is going to be top notch.

"He created and composed a religious thing for the Wesleyan Church on campus for its 75th anniversary—there were 65 trumpets, can you imagine? And I was the Angel Gabriel. He wrote my part and all the others. Everything he does is grandiose and always in good taste. Both he and Dan epitomize what a performance should be."

O'Connor's favorite tune, Dena said, is "Second Hand Rose," an arrangement of which he wrote specially for her. In fact, he has written many arrangements for her including "New York, New York" in what she calls a "pocketbook version." "If you had that done professionally, it would cost at least $75. There's this tiny, little piece of sheet music, so small I could fold it up and put it in my purse. He also wrote 'Second Hand Rose' for me. It was one of the first ones I did for Medicare, and I really like it because the people respond to it." Among O'Connor's other special arrangements for her have been "Bill Bailey Won't You Please Come Home" and "I Can't Give You Anything But Love." But she confesses, most of the time she does torch songs.

Stan Rahn "is my surrogate father," she beams. "He is the steady one, the rock, very dependable. He'll tease me if I have a short skirt on and whisper to me, 'Now, don't forget to sit like a lady.'"

John Bromley, an optometrist by trade and a drummer who played with the big bands years ago, is another favorite of Dena's. "He's a very good drummer. He will often say, 'When I see you shaking, I know I'm playing right.' He really gets me feeling the music, and that's so important."

She calls Don Heitler "a very gifted pianist who is on another plateau above all of us. When I sing with him, I find myself doing things I didn't know I was capable of doing.

"I don't claim to be a musician, but these guys are really good. I've had some schooling, but mostly it's just a love of music. With Donnie, it's his chords. If I were to sing 'Misty' in a certain way, perhaps with someone else, I would be pleased with it. But I wouldn't have reached my ultimate. And with him, I do. He's a true accompanist."

Though Dena and Rahn are often paired as soloists, she says they never practice together. "He'll say, 'Do you know this song?' and I'll say, 'Yeah.' And it's not to say we haven't fallen on our fannies a few times. Jim always said the mistakes are part of the charm of the group, and it sells. I can't think of many other bands where that would work."

EARLE ROBERTS

At 90 years of age, Earle Robert's veined and freckled hands can still pick a mean banjo . . . or a guitar, or a cello, or a bass fiddle, and can glide with grace across the keys of a piano or an organ. Each of these instruments, as well as a prized antique Chinese banjo, which he picked up years ago on the cheap in a Chicago hock shop for $10, occupy special niches in his modest little bungalow on North Franklin Street in Danville.

There isn't much of a hairline left on his nearly bald pate. His tall and slender figure is slightly stooped and he shuffles his bare feet amongst his souvenirs in the parlor as he points with pride to the variety of instruments he continues to use, all neatly arranged along a closet wall like soldiers standing smartly at attention. His mind is sharp and his blue eyes dance behind thick glasses as he relates stories from his past and about his association with Medicare.

Born and reared on Chicago's Southside, Roberts grew up with an almost innate sense of musicality. His mother was a piano teacher, and from the time he was six years old, he has played the ebonies and ivories. Both he and his sister, he said, took lessons from their mother, and were made to practice religously an hour a day. He also became a violinist under the tutelage of a family friend.

A group of his young friends, 11, 12 or 13 years of age (he can't quite remember) got to playing together for their own enjoyment and soon after, for the enjoyment of others at a high school dance "for which I received the magnificent sum of one dollar. From there on I could see that it was a paying proposition, and my musical career started in earnest," he later wrote in a book on music for parents titled, *But Johnny Wouldn't Practice.* Roberts more or less taught himself to play guitar and banjo, and his repertoire also includes the bass and cello.

His talents eventually landed him with different bands with which he played for 20-some years in Chicago hotels, night clubs, and theaters. His eyes twinkled when he recalled one story when he was playing at a Chicago nightclub during the Depression. During the band's intermission, Roberts would stroll among the tables, playing requests from patrons for $1. "This one fellow was obviously a little tipsy," he said, "and came up to me and asked how much I was getting paid to play this tune. I told him 'a dollar,' and he slurred, 'Well, sir, here's one for the request and here's another not to play it."

In the 1930s, Roberts moved up in the world as a staff artist for the CBS and NBC radio networks. Over the next 10 years he played on the "Don McNeil Breakfast Club," "The Carnation Show," "The Armour Hour," and a variety of other radio shows popular during the era. "In playing banjo solos over a major radio network that pulled two to three million listeners, I perhaps have made over a million people happy in one minute of musical effort. This knowledge is a very great reward," he said.

The times, they were a-changin', however. Roberts left the Windy City and some of the glory behind in the '40s after the failure of his first marriage. He traveled around with a three-girl trio, working at various clubs and hotels, among them the Woolford in Danville. The town eventually became his home.

In 1978, Roberts became part of the Medicare entourage. He walked into Dan Perrino's campus office one day to inquire about the possibility of sitting in with the group at one of their concerts, and the rest, as they say, is history.

Perrino, being a shrewd talent scout, was familiar with the Roberts' banjo artistry because he had played for a number of years at a local watering hole, The Village Inn. It didn't take him long to snap up the string-strummer, though there were three other banjo players who would rotate gigs with Roberts for a while. The elderly man with the twinkle in his eye and a gift of musical artistry soon became the darling of the variety of audiences the band played for . . . and a regular performer.

His first gig with Medicare was at a U. of I. Homecoming parade, and soon after, the banjo man was wowing the faithful on the campus and on the road at alumni programs in and out of state.

Among his memorable characteristics is an unfailing sense of humor, and anyone who has ever been on and behind stage with Roberts is aware of the infamous little black book of jokes he always carries with him.

He started writing down jokes in his book back in 1959, he said, hauling out the ragged thing with its yellowed pages in show-and-tell fashion. He keeps the "spicy" ones (for the boys) in the front of the book, and the "clean" ones in the back for the female singers. Dena Vermette laughingly recalled the joke-telling trait that has kept Medicare members in good humor for years.

In 1990, the jokester nearly became a traffic statistic. Perrino said Roberts was driving on the interstate highway from Danville to Champaign for a performance, and in trying to avoid a semi that had stalled on the road, he lost control of his car, which ended up in a ditch. Roberts ended up in the hospital. "John (O'Connor) and I rushed over to the hospital (Roberts was 88 years old at the time), fearing the worst. When we walked into his room, he was lying so still. We quietly walked to the side of his bed, he turned and saw us and said, 'Hey, did you fellas hear the one about. . . ?' John and I turned to each other with a sigh of relief and said, 'Earle's OK.'"

Roberts feels a powerful kinship with his fellow Medicare musicians. "They're like buddies," he said. "Each thing you do with them is a great reward."

At the spry age of 90, Roberts was still playing and still giving music lessons, something he has done for decades. He is proud of "my fledglings who have left the nest and successfully completed the musical requirements in different colleges, emerging with degrees and knowledge which enables them to be full-fledged teachers and fellow workers in this grand task of raising the aesthetic standards of the world in general," he wrote in his book.

"I truthfully can say that my teaching has developed in me the comfortable feeling that comes as a reward to anyone sincerely aspiring to a high type of useful life. I would consider it a compliment of the highest order if the god of music and the arts would someday look down and say, 'Well done, thou good and faithful servant.'"

Earle (with an "e" he emphasizes) Roberts is in a class by himself—a fabulous entertainer, an extremely talented musician, a 'good humor' man, and mostly, a person you're glad you had the good fortune to meet. What a vaudeville team he and George Burns would make!

8

Mr. Medicare: Dan Perrino

His blue eyes crackle behind wire-rimmed glasses with warmth and intelligence, wisps of silver hair are neatly combed across the top of his balding pate, a little mane of it curling up at the nape of his neck. He is moving—always moving—smiling, talking with his hands, planning the next move. He radiates enthusiasm like an aura wherever he goes. In fact, the energy that Dan Perrino packs into his compact, 5'4" frame can only be described as a bit shy of atomic.

At age 72, after "retiring" three times, he is still far from hanging up his many hats—that of "the Godfather" of Medicare, as a leader in the university community (currently as a liaison in the area of cultural diversity for the Alumni Association), and as a volunteer for myriad organizations including mental health, "The Great American People Show" in Springfield, Habitat for Humanity and the Foundation for Educational Excellence in Champaign-Urbana schools. And that is merely the tip of the iceberg.

"Some people think I'm crazy," he muses, but he loves doing for others and being involved—it's made life interesting and fun for him. "We only have one life to live," he said. "Without the university, where could I have had all these experiences? If I had to sit home and didn't have something to do, I'd go nuts. As long as I have something to give, and also receive, I would like to continue to do this."

If anyone is a legend in his own time, it is Dan Perrino. His own humility would cause him to deny such a thing, of course, but it is simply a fact. His genuine love and affection for others and his enthusiasm for life can melt the hardest of hearts and endear him not only to individuals, but multitudes. Being around Perrino is like being caught up in tornado that hugs. And it is also a lesson in the biblical sense—"Do unto others as you would have them do unto you." In a nutshell, that is what Dan Perrino is all about—he has given of himself so unselfishly and cheerfully that he has been unabashedly loved and respected in return.

The cadre of friends he has gathered around the university, the state, and the nation over the years attest to the fact.

Jim Vermette once described Perrino as a person who has "boundless energy, love of people and music, a dynamo. He is loaded with talent. Sometimes you wonder where he's going with his ideas. You think to yourself, 'It can't be done,' but Dan doesn't know the meaning of the word 'can't.' He's wonder man. At times you would think he's disorganized, but he isn't. He's highly organized in his own way."

Former chancellor Jack Peltason said of Perrino when the maestro received the Alumni Association's Distinguished Service Award in the early '80s, "He has counseled students, developed programs for them, lent them money, fed them, worked with them during times of tragedy and during times of triumph. During the late '60s and early '70s he probably did more to keep all of us working together than any single person. All who know Dan wondered in amazement at his apparently boundless energy. I know him well enough and close enough to be aware that at times his own spirits were low and his energy depleted. Yet he never became discouraged and never failed to respond to the call of duty. He was never part of anyone's problems, always a part of everybody's solutions."

Pianist Donny Heitler feels an almost father-brother relationship between himself and Perrino and describes a sense of family within the Medicare organization, which he attributes to his friend.

"Dan stands for love, friendship, quality, honesty, integrity, values, humanity. If he weren't around, there wouldn't be a Medicare. It takes a lot of time, and anyone who writes Danny off as just a busybody and a sax player is just way, way off the mark. Who will send you a birthday card? Danny. Who calls to ask about how things are? Danny. Who brings a jug of cider over for you? He's a real friend. He could ask me to do anything, and I would do it. In his bonding with people, it is next to impossible to say no to him because he wouldn't say no to you."

Dena Vermette can attest to that. "I remember when our girls were little, and I was at home laying on the couch watching TV one night. I was really tired," she recalled, "and the phone rang, and it was Danny. He said Medicare was playing over at Jumer's Hotel in Urbana for the Rotary Club, and wouldn't I come over and sing a couple of songs? 'They'll just love you,' he said. I tell you, he could charm the socks off of you, and as tired as I was, I went over and sang songs and then came home."

Maryo G. Ewell, one-time associate director of the Illinois Arts Council, once wrote, "I know that Dan's heart includes every group of people, every organization, every artist, every child, every individual in Illinois. I am convinced that Dan's brain is behind just about every good new idea in the arts in Illinois. I know that Dan's energy is absolutely devoted to helping people make things happen."

And so it goes. Testimonials, freely given on Perrino's behalf, would, in themselves, fill a book.

ﻌ

Vito Joseph Perrino, the middle child and only son born to Italian immigrants Dominick and Petrina Perrino, was named after his paternal grandfather. It was a name his sister disliked, and when she took him to school for his first day of kindergarten, she introduced him to the principal as "Da . . . Danny." It stuck, but it wasn't until 1982 that the name on his birth certificate was legally changed.

Dan, his parents and his two sisters, lived in a Polish, Lithuanian, and Czechoslovakian melting pot. Theirs was the only Italian family. The other minority in this very blue-collar neighborhood on the West Side of Chicago was an Irish family that lived two doors away. The Perrinos' modest home was situated near what is now Midway Airport and close to the Back of the Yards area near the old stockyards.

Sometimes, growing up was hard in a rough-and-tumble neighborhood for a little boy. "You have to understand," Perrino explained, "that the average education of the fathers in my neighborhood might have been the fourth grade and there was little opportunity (for them) to get any education."

He and his friends always had to be on the lookout for bullies, and when he was in seventh grade he joined a group called the "Dukes," which served a dual purpose—that of a softball team and a neighborhood gang. It was a means of protection, he said. "There was always a lot of pushing and slugging. We seldom walked around, particularly at night, without one or two other members of the gang."

He laughed when he recalled how he used to walk around with rocks in his pocket or carry a big stick just to protect himself. One of the older boys once told him how to protect himself—"If you feel you're gonna get in trouble with the bigger guys, carry a stick and always hit them in the shins and run." Sometimes, he said, he and his friends would get into fights with other boys and the ammunition of choice was tomatoes with rocks in the middle of them.

Another favorite pastime was the old manhole caper. The bigger and stronger boys would lift manhole covers and tell the smaller ones to climb down. The cover would be replaced, and the frightened little boys would search the bottom of the sewers for sticks to which they would affix hankies to poke through the holes, trying to alert passers-by to their plight.

Once when it happened, someone called the police, and the paddywagon arrived late one afternoon just about the time Perrino's father was walking home after alighting from the corner streetcar. When his father saw that a cop was fishing his son out of the sewer, he jokingly told the cop that perhaps he would learn a lesson if he remained in the manhole a little longer.

Later, when walking home with his father, Perrino said everyone in the neighborhood could hear the severe reprimand he got from his dad "whose theory was that it was my responsibility to stay out of trouble."

"One time I was on my way to Goldblatt's department store to buy a tire for my bicycle. The store was on 47th and Ashland, which is right on the corner of Back of the Yards (a much rougher neighborhood). Instead of going down 47th Street, one of the main roadways for cattle trucks on their way to the stock yards, I took 46th Street, a side street, just to get away from the heavy traffic. As I was peddling my bicycle, I looked up and noticed there were a bunch of guys on the corner, and I thought I could avoid them by swinging my bike out and away from them, but of course, I couldn't and they stopped me and took my bicycle. They had BB guns and they told me to run, then started counting to three and shot me in the back. That was the last time I ever veered off the main drag."

But it could also be a chivalrous neighborhood. Friends looked out for friends. As in days of yore, a champion could be chosen as a stand-in for the duel of the day. Being smaller than the others, if he happened to get into a fight, "I could choose someone bigger than me to fight for me, and I always picked my cousin who was big and a good fighter. That was the entertainment of the day," he laughed. "You'd go to an empty lot and stand around and watch the fights."

Being Italian, the whole family was always interested in music. His father enjoyed singing a little opera for his own entertainment, but no one had any formal musical training. When Perrino was in sixth grade, he heard a performance by a WPA orchestra at Richard Edwards Elementary School. "That's when I first became interested in music," he said, and he was really impressed when he got to talk to the musicians after the concert.

When he was six years old, he attended what he termed "my first musical event" when his father took him to see an opera, "La Forza del Destino" by Giuseppe Verdi at the old Auditorium in Chicago. "We sat in the upper, upper, upper balcony, and it cost 25 cents to get in."

As time passed, his father would always find enough money, even though it was during the Depression and he sometimes only earned as little as $8 a week, to periodically take the family to a vaudeville show or a movie. When Perrino was about eight years old, his father took him to the Tivoli Theater on the city's South Side to see Guy Lombardo's orchestra. "All the saxophone players were sitting in the front row of the orchestra, and I decided then and there that was what I wanted to do—play one of those shiny saxophones." As time went on, he saw many of the big bands—Glenn Miller, Duke Ellington, Harry James, Benny Goodman.

"I was saturated with that all my young life, and though I played a lot of softball, most of my early existence was playing music."

A professor of music and friend of his father's, Joseph Partillo, gave the young horn player his first music lessons. He remembers starting with lessons called "solfeggio," a method of learning to sight-sing. "One would sing the notes, using the syllables do, re, mi, etc., and it taught you to read music."

After about a year with Partillo, "He asked me if we had a piano at home. I said we didn't, and he told me if I wanted to learn how to play music, I would have to learn how to play the piano.

"I told him I didn't want to play piano, I wanted to play the saxophone. He blew up because he didn't consider the saxophone to be a legitimate instrument for study, and he wouldn't talk to me for a month."

That's when Perrino began studying at Hull House, the settlement house started by Jane Addams, where Benny Goodman began his music instruction some 10 years earlier. At his first recital he played "The Boulevard of Broken Dreams" on a $25 soprano saxophone "that was too heavy for me to hold up, so I had to rest it as I was playing on a little bench."

By the time he was 12, Perrino had acquired his first instrument. Shortly afterward, he began playing saxophone in the Kelly High School band. One day, someone broke into his locker and stole all of his books and his horn. "The principal said I had to pay for the books, and I asked him who was going to pay for the saxophone. He said I was, and I told him he was crazy if he thought I was going to pay for my stolen books and he wasn't going to pay for the horn. Well, as soon as I foolishly called him 'crazy,' he slapped me and my knee-jerk reaction was to kick him in the leg and run. So after some discussion, he thought it would be best if I went to another school, so I went to Tilden Tech and that took care of that."

Tilden turned out to be a whole new ballgame for the pint-sized teenager. The large, all-boys school was smack dab in the middle of enemy territory in the rough Back of the Yards neighborhood. Perrino said he got involved in another altercation with some of the school bullies who started chasing him. "There was a three-foot fence that other kids could hand-spring over with no problem, and I was always jealous because I couldn't do it." When the chase was on, he remembers clearing that three-foot fence like it wasn't even there.

"I kept running until I came to an intersection and saw a policeman. I went up to him and stayed there, waiting for the bullies to go away, but they didn't, so I just followed the cop until I could jump on a streetcar and go home."

Petrified to go back to class, Perrino cut school for 78 days, unbeknownst to his parents. He hid in movie theaters, and said, "I saw 'Captain Blood' at least 15 or 16 times . . . I knew all the lines." Eventually his sister, who had been covering for him, arranged a meeting between her brother and his homeroom teacher, and he was transferred back to Kelly. To his relief, a new principal was in charge.

He rejoined the school band and at the end of his junior year, was its president. At the director's request, Perrino formed a dance band, and they played for the school's variety show and school dances.

Perrino's first professional performance in a band was at the age of 13 when he played his sax with a drummer and an accordionist on New Year's Eve at a tavern on Kedzie and Archer Streets. "We played from 9:30 p.m. to 6:30 a.m., and my father sat there through the whole thing. I was paid $3 and thought I was a millionaire. I was bitten by the bug."

Soon after, one of his cousins, another Vito Perrino, played a major role in the youngster's early music education. The older Vito was also a saxophonist and invited his little cousin to sit in on engagements he had at church socials. The more he played, the better he got, enough so that he became comfortable performing for dances during those developing years.

At age 16, Perrino, "62 inches of Swing," was playing in a sextet at a variety of small nightclubs, one of which was the Horseshoe Lounge in Cicero. "It was rumored that Al Capone was the owner," Perrino recalled. There was gambling downstairs and prostitution upstairs, "though I was too naive to know about that at the time. We were playing and all of a sudden the manager of the club came up to us and said, 'In about 15 minutes we're gonna be raided, but don't be nervous, just sit there.' So we did, and when the cops came in, I was petrified because my mother didn't know I was playing in a place like that." The musicians were passed over in the roundup, but the second time the place was raided, they were hauled off to the lockup. "My dad didn't know anything about that until several years later," Perrino said with a sigh.

He once played in a 22-piece pit orchestra at the Rialto Burlesque Theater, "legitimate burlesque," Perrino insisted. "It wasn't sleazy," he said. "The top comedians like Red Skelton, Danny Thomas, Bob Hope, and George Burns played there in earlier times. I remember we had to wear tuxes. I was only 16 at the time, and when the school principal found out about it, she made me quit because she thought it was a scandal."

When he got back to school, all of his boy friends crowded around him, full of curiosity and eagerly inquiring, "What did ya see, what did ya see?," meaning the strippers. "They couldn't believe I didn't see a thing cuz I was concentrating so hard on the music." He added that legitimate burlesque was a cleaner show than many of the shows featured on television and today's motion pictures.

ð.

Neither of Perrino's parents were formally educated, but his bricklayer father was self-taught, and his mother was a dressmaker in the garment district of Chicago for the Vogue Company. They were proud parents; proud of their heritage and hard workers. And both were determined their son would have a college education. His older sister had died at the age of 17 from pneumonia, and he hardly knew the younger one who died when she was a baby. There was always the understanding that at least one member of the family would better himself through higher education.

As it was, the young Perrino had had enough of the insecurity of the entertainment business anyway. The band had been hitting the resort circuit and playing at ballrooms like Melody Mill and O Henry, and were always running out of money for food and gasoline.

In the spring of 1940, he enrolled at the University of Chicago and the Chicago Musical College but soon after decided that he needed another approach to his music education. During the same period, he heard the University of Illinois Concert Band conducted by A. Austin Harding and "I was so knocked out by the performance, I decided then and there that's where I wanted to continue my education."

The marquee at the renowned Krannert Center for the Performing Arts said it all. In late winter 1976, Medicare, sponsored by student organization Star Course, played to a sell-out crowd.

D ick Cisne tickled the ivories and John O'Connor plugged in his trumpet mute as the band warmed up for its first Dads Night performance at the Thunderbird restaurant, Urbana, 1971.

R ockin' through the years—In 1974, Medicare 7, 8 or 9 posed on the stage at the Krannert Center prior to the band's first trip out of state to perform for U. of I. alumni in California. Pictured are Dick Cisne (piano); D. Perrino (saxophone); Robert Parkinson (trombone); John O'Connor (trumpet Rudy James (drums); Dan Perantoni (bass tuba); Stan Rahn (clarinet); and Morgan Powell (trombone).

Ahoy, mates! The band was piped aboard a U.S. aircraft carrier in San Diego harbor, compliments of alumnus and shipmate Lt. Joe Rank, during the 1974 California tour. Left to right: Ron Riddle, Rudy James, John O'Connor and an airman.

The one and only George Shearing (left) and his friend, Medicare pianist Donny Heitler, entertain fans in the South Lounge of the Illini Union in 1973.

T he first of many half-time performances (this one in 1972) during
Illinois football games.

B rown-baggers in Chicago's Loop gathered by the thousands for a
series of noon-time Medicare concerts at the First National Bank
Plaza during the summer of 1978. Here, the gang wraps up their signa-
ture "When the Saints Go Marching In."

On the road . . . During the infamous 1979 trip to Washington, D.C., an ice storm stranded the group in Atlanta for three days. Shown here, stalwart travelers (from back to front) Morgan Powell; Dan Perantoni; Ray Sasaki; Dan Perrino, Dena and Jim Vermette (director of the Alumni Association); Harry Ruedi, and Dick Cisne.

Many cities around the state of Illinois have welcomed performances by the Medicare band. Here, Dan Perrino, Dena Vermette, and Carlyle Johnson pose prior to a special concert in Quincy, Johnson's hometown.

D an Perrino leads the band into the lobby of the Krannert Center for the Performing Arts to entertain members and directors of the U. of I. Foundation at their annual fall meeting in Urbana.

S tan Rahn and Dena Vermette croon it up at the annual benefit concert at Willowbrook High School in Villa Park, Illinois. The band has performed at the school for 20 years, raising money to assist high school dropouts.

Ten years young—John O'Connor, Dan Perrino, Stan Rahn and Mo Carter get ready to cut the cake in the South Lounge of the Illini Union in November 1979, on the tenth anniversary of Medicare's inception.

J amming with the house band at Disneyland during Medicare's first California tour.

A ir Force Gen. Norma Brown got a rousing send-off by the Medicare band on the occasion of her retirement as the commanding officer of Chanute Air Force Base in Rantoul, Illinois.

E arle Roberts, at age 92, is the oldest member of the band and is still wowing audiences with his jazz renditions on the banjo. He continues to give music lessons to youngsters on a variety of musical instruments at his home in Danville.

D anville optometrist Dr. John Bromley grooves on his drums during a rehearsal with fellow musicians Ray Sasaki on trumpet and Dick Cisne on piano.

"R ev." Stan Rahn croons and woos the ladies during a summer concert sponsored by the Rockford Park District.

In 1984 Illinois went to the Rose Bowl, and Medicare 7, 8 or 9 happily went along, entertaining more than 20,000 U. of I. fans at the huge tailgate party outside the stadium in Pasadena.

John O'Connor has masterminded many of the band's educational concerts over the years, including those for elementary school children. Here he astounds his young audience by playing two trumpets at the same time.

Left to right: Gregg Helgeson, Carl Johnson, Dena Vermette, Dan Perrino, Donny Heitler and John O'Connor warm up for a three-day swing around the state that took the band to Quincy, Belleville, and the Illinois State Fair in Springfield.

Former Illinois governor James Thompson presented Dan Perrino with the Governor's Award at ceremonies in Chicago in 1982 in recognition of Medicare's spirit of volunteerism shown in their performances for schools, senior citizens, and others. (Photo by Don Craig

N o topping-off party would be complete without a little Dixieland jazz. Medicare was happy to oblige at the topping-off ceremonies for the multi-million dollar Beckman Institute on the campus of the University of Illinois in August 1987. Back row: Don Percival, Russ Pence, Carl Johnson, Donny Heitler, Erik Lund and Bill Olson. Front row: Dennis Wiziecki, Dan Perrino, Paul Dixon, and Earle Roberts.

G ov. Jim Edgar (center) and U. of I. President Stanley O. Ikenberry shared the stage with the band for an alumni function at the Illinois State Fair in 1991.

W hen George Burns brought his show to the Assembly Hall during Homecoming in the fall of 1992, Medicare 7, 8 or 9 got the call, as they have so many times for other entertainers, to do the warm-up for the show. Posing with the comedian back stage are John O'Connor, John Bromley, Dan Perrino, Mo Carter, Dena Vermette, Paul Rainey, Earle Roberts, and Carl Johnson.

F ormer high school band director Warren Felts cu his teeth on Dixieland in Ne Orleans, playing on the Mississippi Queen and Delt Queen paddlewheel riverboats.

H arry Ruedi belts one out as Mo Carter goes solo at one of many Rockford Park District concerts.

F ormer U. of I. faculty member Dan Perantoni, now a professor at Arizona State University, blew a mean tuba with Medicare for many years before moving to the southwest.

The man himself—"Mr. Medicare," Dan Perrino.

The following fall, Perrino enrolled at Illinois. He happily immersed himself in the School of Music and the ROTC with the war looming on the horizon. Two and one-half years later he, and so many other young men like him, put their educations on hold to answer the call of Uncle Sam. Perrino joined the service and was shipped off to the Pacific Theater in the Philippines, where he became a behind-the-lines communications officer with the 77th Division.

Besides his military duties, Perrino found time to teach and entertain. As the war was ending, his commanding general, who happened to be a former ROTC officer at the U. of I., learned that Perrino had been a music major. The general introduced the young officer to a special service officer who asked Perrino to organize a musical group and tour Japan to entertain the troops. The show, with music and vaudeville, toured the country for six months after the surrender of Japan.

"I remember we were getting ready to leave on the train for Sapporo. There had been a foul-up. We were supposed to have a reserved car for all 22 band members, performers, and our instruments, but it turned up full of Japanese civilians. And you have to remember at that time, Japanese railroad cars ran on narrow gauge tracks and were much, much smaller than American ones, so things were pretty tight. Well, the Japanese travel master wanted to pull all of these people out of the car so we could board, but I told my interpreter that perhaps we could all fit."

The band members and their instruments squeezed in with the Japanese contingent, and "it was terribly crowded," Perrino recalled. A lot of the natives had to stand and were not at all happy about being displaced by a bunch of GIs and band equipment. "It was a pretty tense situation," said Perrino. "We really didn't know what to expect."

The musicians began to talk about music. "Pretty soon, one of them hauled out his guitar and started strumming it to demonstrate a certain chord progression. Then, out came other instruments—a clarinet and a string bass player—and pretty soon we had a jam session going. When the music started, it just broke the tension. Smiles started to break out on the faces of the Japanese, and before we knew it, all this food—cookies and stuff—started coming to us."

Before returning stateside, Perrino organized community music groups and taught American music to Japanese children, an experience that would change his musical ambitions from that of a player to that of a teacher.

One particular experience in the Land of the Rising Sun will forever be cherished, Perrino said. "I was introduced to a woman who had a music degree from Temple University who had organized a Japanese women's chorus in Hakodate, Hokkaido.

"As we became better acquainted, we thought it would be nice if we could expand her women's chorus to a full mixed chorus of both men and women. The merged chorus numbered about 120 voices and brought together the women with GIs from the 77th Division."

The first and only performance was held on Christmas morning in a Christian church. Huge snowflakes gently fell to the ground as the men walked to the church. The contrast between their olive drab attire and the colorful kimonos of the Japanese was striking. Perrino remembered the Army chaplain sermonizing in English while Reverend Kusama interpreted in Japanese to the natives.

"The children were delightful, especially when Santa entered the church and all of the GIs sang 'Jingle Bells' followed by other carols. It was just a few months after the surrender, and we didn't have access to toys or other appropriate gifts. But, in their own inimitable way, the GIs improvised by wrapping objects they had in their possession—Hershey bars, matches, razor blades, stationery, C-rations—in colorful paper and placed them under the tree. The Japanese had so little at the time. There were many tears on the faces of those hardened combat soldiers . . . it was just all so very special."

By the time Perrino returned to the States, he had made up his mind that he wanted to teach music. He finished his master's degree and, in 1949, a year after marrying his college sweetheart and fellow sax player, Marjorie Galutia, whom he met in a psychology class, he became director of instrumental music for the Macomb public school system. Two years later, he held the same position at Quincy. In 1955, he returned to Urbana as director of music in the Urbana school system.

In 1960, he joined the U. of I. faculty as an assistant professor in music extension, and by 1961 he was head of the department as well as director of the Illinois Summer Youth Music Program, in which 1,600 gifted high school students from 18 states participated.

In the late '50s and early '60s, Perrino was still blowing his own horn with local bands like Johnny Bruce, but in 1960, a skiing accident came close to ending his playing career.

His left arm was paralyzed and he was hospitalized for a month at the U. of I. Hospital in Chicago with a slipped disc. The story goes that shortly after entering the hospital he was placed in a large circular room with about 35 other patients. Fourteen men in white marched in the room and surrounded his bed. The resident surgeon looked at the clip board at the bottom of the bed and noted that Perrino was an assistant professor of music. The doctor's first question was not "How are you feeling?" or "Where does it hurt?" but, "Are you a card-carrying member of the musicians union?"

Perrino, suffering a great deal of pain, remembers being stunned by such a question, but answered, "Yes, but I don't understand." The doctor's response was, "If you have surgery, your doctor will be Dr. Eric Oberg who is president of the Chicago Symphony Orchestra Board." It seems the symphony was on strike at the time and had been causing the board all kinds of grief.

One of Perrino's former students from Urbana High School, D.L. Havens, occasionally stopped by to visit and would bring him the newspaper. He read one day that the strike had ended, and that Dr. Oberg and Mayor Richard Daley and his wife would attend a concert together. After Oberg finished his examination that day, Perrino mentioned in passing, "Say hello to the Daleys for me."

The word had somehow gotten around Perrino's ward that he was a friend of the mayor. In truth, there was a warm family relationship between the Daleys and the senior Perrinos. Dan's father had done some work on the Daley home in Bridgeport and their summer home in Michigan, and his mother had not only made some of Sis Daley's dresses, but had entertained the mayor and his wife at some of her famous Italian feasts in the Perrino home.

To his great surprise, Perrino was suddenly whisked out of his big room into a private room. Completely mystified, he asked the nurse why. She retorted, "Well, aren't you somebody important?" He remembers saying, "'No, I don't think so,'" and then she said, "'There's this big box of candy and flowers out there from the mayor's office.'"

Perrino said he couldn't stand the private room, however, because there was no television or radio, and asked to be transferred back to his old room.

Eventually, after a lot of physical therapy, the man with the golden horn was able to resume playing.

૨ª

In 1968, a year before Medicare was formed, Perrino was named dean of student programs and services, a position he held until 1976. During that time he coordinated more than 60 programming units on the campus, many of which are currently established in other units of the university such as the Black Chorus, the Afro-American Dance Team and Percussion Ensemble, La Casa Cultural Latina, Quad Day, and the University Forum for Current Affairs.

In 1976 he wanted to return to academe and the arts, and was made associate dean of the College of Fine Arts, a position he "retired" from in 1988. He retired from the University in 1989, but then accepted a position as alumni liaison for the School of Music and development. He "retired" the third time in 1992, then immediately joined the staff at the Alumni Association, where he currently coordinates all of Medicare's activities and spearheads a cultural diversity program and organizes events and activities for retired alumni and faculty.

Dan Perrino has been recognized for his devotion, not only to music, but also to his fellow man, countless times over the years. Awards from the city of Champaign, the Varsity "I" Association, the Champaign-Urbana *News-Gazette,* Boy Scouts of America, the Latino alumni, the black community, the Alumni Association, the governor of the state, the Illinois Arts Council, the service clubs (Rotary, Lions, Exchange), and many more attest to his devotion, vigor, and everlasting gift of himself to others.

Perrino believes strongly that the arts are not frills. "It's man's culture and its expression in the arts that keeps him together, that gives him soul," he once said. He also said that "People are lonely because they build walls instead of bridges."

By all accounts, this dynamic Italian music-maker and ambassador extraordinaire is undoubtedly one of the world's greatest bridge builders.

9

The Magic

Back in 1969, university administrators and faculty might have thought that some sort of sorcery or supernatural powers were at work, hidden in the notes or lyrics of the tunes Medicare played. What else could explain the transformation taking place before their unbelieving eyes—a simple dialog of Dixieland music was successful in diffusing the distrust and opening the clogged lines of communication on a campus on the brink of revolution. After all, in more modern times, some rock groups have been accused of practicing the black arts subliminally through their craft.

But the real magic of Medicare does not fall into the first few of Webster's Dictionary's definitions of the word such as "possessing supernatural powers; sorcerous; any pretended or supposed supernatural art," but rather in a second definition— "Any agency that works with wonderful effect."

To the thousands of people who have heard Medicare play over the years—young and old, friends or strangers, the effect has been wonderful, surprising and enduring. And that raises the question, "Why?"

We asked Gregg "Dr. Freud" Helgesen, trumpet player with Medicare and clinical psychologist, to put on his white coat and lay Medicare on the couch for an in-depth analysis. It didn't take more than a second. "It's Dan," he said, "his ability to be a peacemaker. He doesn't like any kind of animosity. He's always diplomatic."

Others, either in the group or connected in some way with it, echoed Helgesen's analysis.

Jim Vermette said, "I think Dan is the key. I think it's a love of the music, the love of the people, the love of performing and knowing that they are appreciated. They feel as though they are doing a real service, not only for the university, but for the kind of music they play.

"Some of the musicians think that this kind of music needs to be perpetuated, and that they carry on a legacy in a way. It's interesting how many young musicians have played with them, and that's one of the great things about its being a university program. It's not just pure music, which is fun, but they educate the audience about the music, about the composers, about the history—about it being such a part of Americana. Jazz is so much American; every part of our culture has participated in it."

Vermette also contends that the personalities of the musicians make the group magical. "It's the chemistry of the group that opens other people up. They reach out and people know they are around nice folks. A lot of musical groups just go through the motions, but these guys have heart and soul.

"To be truly great, I believe, you've got to have passion. You gotta get into it to be great, and I think Medicare is truly great because they feel the music. They're doing it because they love it, and they're not in it for the money.

"It's the giving endeavor, and that comes across. They're not going through the motions. They're playing because they love it, and they love people, and that's a combination that's hard to beat."

Donny Heitler said, "Dan is really better than he needs to be in taking care of people," which includes people in the band. "Dan's leadership communicates the sense of bonding that has occurred with the Medicare organization and the music represents that.

"Then there's this concept that we don't rehearse; we just show up and start playing," he said. "We don't care. What's a wrong note among friends? What's a bad joke among friends? It's always good humor and positive in a way. That's the magic of it. A pro would look at that and say, 'That's buffoonery!' I don't know of any other group like it. They take it seriously, but not so seriously that they can't have fun."

John O'Connor thinks Medicare's popularity has endured because "We have fun, and people are looking for fun. They don't want to be stymied with formality. They just want to relax. This kind of music is relaxing and we enjoy playing it and we relax—more than an organized group does that rehearses and has to play spit and polish on their charts. But we don't get hung up when we make mistakes. We laugh them off. The people know when we make a mistake, and we laugh and make fun of it.

"But we have enough quality to persevere," he insists. "It's musicianship. There are tremendously talented musicians in here who can go formal and can play with the best of them. And they join our group with that same feeling . . . 'Well, here's a group that we don't have to worry about (being so formal), and we'll just come and have fun.'

"And there's the camaraderie which is important among the men and the women that's developed into a fellowship—a fraternity or sorority kind of thing. But the main reason it still goes on is because of that credo—we get together to entertain for various purposes and all of those purposes are basically noble ones."

"There's never any ego trip among these guys," said Stan Rahn. "We feel comfortable playing with each other because there's excellent musicianship, and Dan is skillful in pulling people together. He gives every person a chance to shine at his expense. He is very modest with his own horn. He's skillful at establishing rapport with an audience. He can read an audience quickly. And because he is tiny, smaller, I think that has some effect. If he was 6'4", it would be different. I think people just feel like he's a teddy bear and put their arms around him.

"Sometimes you get a little ticked off at him because we're supposed to knock off at a certain time and he'll say we have to draw this thing to a close. And some of the guys will say, 'Let's put our horns away; we've done enough,' but we'll do another couple of numbers and the audience loves it. He's a master showman in a quiet way."

Helgesen also agrees that the warm relationships among the musicians carries over to the audience "to the extent that we are able to remain spontaneous and that we make sure that we have fun. We don't see it as a job very often, and as long as we don't, then we can enjoy ourselves and I think that probably translates, particularly when someone is on a roll . . . when Morgan (Powell) is playing or saying things that are funny.

"We're always trying to sabotage Dan in some way . . . playing tricks on him like making side comments and trying to crack him up so that he blows his introduction on the next tune. He takes it in good grace."

Another reason for the magic of Medicare is because of their dedication to 'pass it on'—integrating younger musicians with the older ones.

Heitler said, "Medicare is basically a pool of very good musicians, but there is a variance in quality and talent level. The old guard is wonderful, but I see the younger players come, and Dan has a way of integrating them into the Medicare concept and that puts a little different spin on it. But there again, that's Dan and his ability to relate to them and what he would like to see them do in terms of the overall Medicare focus."

Helgesen explained, "As we bring in new people, they bring in new tunes and new ways of thinking about things, and we get a creative input. After you play with the same people over and over again, you start hearing the same melodies they're hearing, and you start playing note for note what they might play. So it's nice having enough people that there is always something different going on."

Helgesen also believes that there is a special connection between Medicare and its audiences that may not exist between other musical groups and their audiences.

"There's a closeness in the band that has developed, and that closeness sends a message to the audience," he said. "That audience is there voluntarily. No one has twisted their arms to come and see us, so there is always a connection. Especially so for the older alumni and retirees. They all remember Stan and Mo and John and Dan from when they were in school, so that's an automatic rapport. The rest of us may not know all of these people, though we may know some of them. But I don't think there's anyone in Medicare who has the memory that Dan has. Someone will have to get it all on a pocket-size computer," he laughed.

In fact, Helgesen compared Perrino's mind to a parallel-processing computer. "He's very single-minded, which has always surprised me, because if you watch him operate, he seems to be going off on different tracks all the time, and you wouldn't think anything was going to get done, but it does."

Vermette recalled also thinking at times that Perrino was disorganized because he always seems to have so many balls in the air at the same time and goes at such a dizzying pace. But he isn't disorganized, Vermette said, "He's highly organized in his own way. He's a wonder man."

Vermette also sees magic in other members of the old guard. John O'Connor, for instance, is a "very creative, dynamic, lovable person who has lots of energy and plays with his whole body." Wife Dena, thinks O'Connor is key to the group and represents the real message of Medicare. "He puts his whole body into his music and communicates a flare and a presence of joy to the audiences."

Stan Rahn is "the rock," said both Vermettes. "He's just solid," said Jim. "He's confident, street-smart, has a great voice. He's Mr. Smooth." To Dena, Rahn represents a surrogate father.

Vermette characterizes Mo Carter as "a character with lots of personality. He has a lively leg when he plays, and is virtually the model of a Dixieland player. And, being from the South, he can fit right in with any New Orleans group."

On Art Proteau—"He's a real performer on the banjo and as a singer. He has real personality on the stage, and is a very smart guy."

On Earle Roberts—"He's a total pro; a real presence on the stage. Earle is one of those show-stopper performers and one of the best storytellers I've ever known. He has presence and charm."

On Donny Heitler—"He's talented, smart, and gifted." Dena added, "Donny is on another plateau above all of us. When I sing with him, I find myself doing things I didn't know I was capable of."

Hugh Satterlee's analysis of Medicare's magic is that "It's elementally toe-tapping music. It's easy to whistle, to hum, it's easy to rhythmically get involved in." In the beginning, he said, "When the pianist was grinning the whole time, when the drummer was having a great time, that was fun and they did it in a traditional way which gave everybody performing an opportunity to do a solo. That was the way they played their Dixieland—

it was something the students could relate to. And I guess in my own mind, it provided two things . . . that you could be an individual, yet work as a team.

"It was designed to attract students; it attracted older people, and subsequently it has become almost a talisman for the university and its alumni. It pulls the alums back to the university. It has always been that style of music with Dan. What you see is what you get. There is nothing hidden.

"We not only brought the alumni close to the university (through Medicare), we got a different kind of image. A very informal, fun-like image from people who had nothing to do with the U. of I. They still do it for fun. They don't gain anything financially from it, and everybody admires them for it."

Tuba player Dan Perantoni told a *News-Gazette* reporter once, "Dan gives us all respect and makes it fun. Without him we wouldn't have stayed together all these years. You know musicians are out to make a buck when they perform, but Danny makes you want to do it for nothing."

Perhaps Willard Broom summed it up the best. "Dan always talked about a basic faith that the arts really do bring people together, and music is one of the arts that does it best. And he really believes that. It's a guiding principle of his life. When you combine the power of music with the desire to bring people together, it really can be magical."

ᘒ

Twenty-three years and counting! And the question inevitably arises, can the band survive without Dan Perrino?

Gregg Helgesen pondered the question before answering. "Not as we know it, not the least of which reason is the logistics of it are too much for one person to run out of a house. Whoever did it would have to be sponsored, probably someone with a university connection who had an office to work out of because the number of requests we get per year is just phenomenal. Unless there's someone at the university or that's university-affiliated who is willing to put into it all the work that Danny does, it won't survive as we know it. And that may be appropriate because it is so much him. He'll deny that, but everybody knows it."

This Medicare "concept," which began in 1969 as a group of eight faculty members and graduate students continues to mushroom in number of performers and performances. Invitations for the band to perform pour in by the hundreds every year from every corner of the country, many more than Perrino can possibly accept. Their special magic has permeated the band's own ranks and has spread to its audiences wherever they may be—in a schoolroom, at an alumni gathering, on a riverboat or an aircraft carrier, in a park or on a football field, in church or in concert halls.

As far as Mr. Medicare, Dan Perrino, is concerned, it's all for a good cause. The infectious nature of the music will continue to entertain the band's audiences in live performances as well as occasional television appearances, and will live on for fans through the audio magic of cassette tapes and compact discs.

"As long as we have teeth and breath and people are listening," said Perrino, "we will continue to play."

And when all the saints go marchin' in, you can bet that Medicare 7, 8 or 9 will be among that number, rootin' and tootin' their horns, tickling the ivories, strumming banjos and basses, and creating heavenly smiles and a joyous chorus every step of the way.

Epilogue

Well, what's next? This book has ended, but Medicare seems to roll on and on. I must remind you that the band does not promote itself. We have no marketing plans or program, no press kit, no ads in magazines or newspapers. Other than being listed in the Illinois Arts Council's *Arts Tours* publication, there are no other listings. Our performances result from special requests, and the reasons for this are simple. We are not in the business of becoming a commercial group outside of what we do for the university and our own immediate community. Besides, all the musicians have other responsibilities. Some lead their own ensembles, others play with other jazz units, all of which can present conflicts when trying to schedule performances on a regular basis. We have been asked to do so, but for some, teaching loads and other university-related duties would prevent this. The same is true for those not associated with the university, but who have full-time careers of their own as businessmen, lawyers, doctors, engineers, etc. Thus, University of Illinois commitments remain our top priority.

And here must be the first of my bundle of "thank yous"— to all of those musicians who, through the years, have continued to be a part of whatever we do. In the 23 years of the band's existence, no one has ever pulled out because they did not want to be a part of the Medicare tradition. There were and are times when someone has a schedule conflict and cannot make a performance, but never because he or she did not enjoy involvement with our efforts.

As you have already read, most of the musicians who perform on a somewhat regular basis live in the immediate campus area. They number about 35. However, as we travel to different parts of the state or around the nation, we call on musicians we know who live in those areas to join our ranks. This is always a happy occasion because it becomes a kind of reunion or homecoming as well as a performance for an alumni audience.

Not all of the musicians are necessarily close friends, but there is a special bonding among them that is interesting to observe. The age span of the group, as of this writing, is 22 to 92. Yet, when we are together, whether for performances or picnics, there is almost a oneness that exists. Perhaps if we performed together every night, this might not be the case. But presently, we do enjoy being with each other and seeing old friends as we come together to perform.

Just as there are age differences, there are also different levels of performance. Those who play with some degree of regularity, obviously are the stronger musicians. We look up to them and, I must say, capitalize on their skills. They never seem to look down on those of us who haven't had as many performing opportunities or are getting up in age.

But regardless of the levels of experience, each musician makes his or her own contribution to the ensemble at a given time. So whatever their age or their experience in jazz might be, I personally am grateful to each and every one who has given of their time and talent so unselfishly to the Medicare cause and to the university. Without them there would be no Medicare.

Some of you are already familiar with Medicare. But you may not be aware of what happens when we receive an invitation to perform for a function or event. You should know at the outset that, as mentioned earlier, we do not seek engagements, not because it is beneath us, but because that is not our function. Our primary mission is to enhance the good will of the university and to perform for alumni across the country. Thus, there are enough requests to keep us busy.

When we do receive a call or an inquiry, I look over our list of musicians and select seven, eight, or nine who I believe would fit in with the particular program. Then I write each of them a letter telling them about the invitation and ask if they can participate. I enclose a self-addressed and stamped postcard that allows the musician to indicate whether he or she is available. When the cards are returned, if someone indicates they are unable to attend, I go on to the next musician on my list until the ensemble is complete. Generally speaking, we can accept close to 90 percent of our invitations, especially if we receive them four to six months in advance.

For me, the musical experience is only a part of the joy of being associated with this great group of individuals. Each personality is unique, and in every group there are comedians. Some of the incidents that have occurred over time are truly unforgettable.

One such was a performance we gave for a group of Champaign-Urbana teachers—a recognition event. As I have already said, we do not rehearse, but if we are performing something new, we do so "live" before our audience, informing them, of course, that this is the case. On this particular occasion, I had asked vocalist Dena Vermette if she was familiar with the words. This was all stated in front of the audience and over the sound system. We keep no secrets from our listeners.

Dena turned toward the back of the ensemble and said, as she began walking, "I'll need my glasses in order to see the words. And by the way, I just bought a new pair—from Osco—paid $7.95 for them." She reached into her purse and pulled out the glasses and put them on. Then, as she walked back to the front of the stage, she fitted them properly and said, as she looked both to the audience and to the band, "How do they look?" I said, "great," that the glasses even raised her IQ by at least 20 points. Russ Pence, our trumpet player that day, blurted out, "Well, that gets it up to 70."

The teachers enjoyed this bit of impromptu humor as did the band members and, as usual, it brought the two groups—the audience and the band—closer together. It's this type of intimacy that we enjoy and work toward whether through our music or through the bantering on stage.

Another story I'd like to share with you happened when we were in San Francisco and were returning from a performance for the Palo Alto Illini Club to the beautiful St. Francis Hotel on Union Square. It was late Friday evening and the elevator was crowded with guests returning from a night out. Included among those on the elevator were myself and other band members Morgan Powell and Harry Ruedi, plus our wives.

To begin with, you should know that Morgan, a faculty member in the U. of I.'s School of Music, is originally from Texas and, as you might expect, quite a casual fellow. Making a fashion statement is not on Morgan's list of priorities, but before leaving for the tour, his wife had insisted that he purchase a new sport coat, which he did. Harry, on the other hand, had been a haberdasher with Hart Shaffner and Marx for many years, and is a very stylish dresser.

Our little group had eaten dinner earlier that evening at a very expensive Italian restaurant, and while munching on his salad, Morgan had spilled salad oil on the sleeve of his new sport coat.

While riding up in the elevator, Harry took a long look at Morgan's coat and said softly, though everyone in the elevator could hear clearly, "That's a new sport coat, Morgan, isn't it?" To which Morgan quietly responded after a moment of silence, "Yes. I paid $10 for it at a factory outlet." Harry asked, "What's that spot on your coat?" Morgan replied, "Oh, I spilled some salad oil on my coat at the restaurant." Another pause and more silence in the elevator, for by this time everyone was curious about the conversation between the two. Finally, Harry piped up, "Hell, you got a $12 spot on a $10 coat," at which time the elevator exploded with laughter.

I must also extend very special thanks to those musicians who are not on the university payroll, but take time from their varied job responsibilities and places of business to perform with us on campus and on the road. Most of our out-of-state tours are 12 days to two weeks in length, and some of the band members must take as many days off from work in order for us to complete our tour responsibilities.

I am sure you will agree that this is a major effort that requires some sacrifice and, in some instances, a loss of income. These include optometrist Dr. John Bromley; clinical psychologist Dr. Gregg Helgeson; Dr. Woody Woodward, professor of anatomy and biology at Parkland College; Bob Towner with Lincoln Trail Library; Russ Pence, a marketing executive; Dennis Wiziecki, an advertising manager for Research Press; Jack May, owner and manager of May True Value Hardware; and Don Heitler, a professional musician whose sole income is from his musical performances.

And how could we forget to thank our wives?—especially mine, since I do much of my telephoning and paper work at home. They are ever so patient while we are away performing. But some do travel with us on extended tours, and they are always welcomed and are a blessing, for not only do they take care of us, but they help us with equipment, keep us on schedule, keep track of our luggage, and even serve as travel guides.

Beverly Bromley has made more trips with us than any of the other spouses, and she has proven to be very helpful in locating good restaurants and is our road map specialist. Whenever we are lost, Beverly can find the solution to our dilemma and get us back on track.

We are also very grateful to so many departments on campus. Whenever we need assistance of any kind, there always seems to be someone who can help us.

There are so many individuals on the campus who, in their own special ways, have assisted us that I find it almost impossible to list them all; technicians in the School of Music, the Motor Pool, staff and faculty from all corners of the campus, and of course, University administrators.

But I must single out Jack McKenzie, retired dean of the College of Fine and Applied Arts, Robert Bays and Austin McDowell, both retired directors of the School of Music. They are important, as well as Hugh Satterlee, former vice-chancellor of student affairs, for they provided a "home" as a place to administer Medicare activities and performances. And also thanks to Willard Broom, associate dean of students for his talents not only as an efficient "gofer," but also as a "perceptive consultant" on student feelings and desires. We are most grateful.

I especially want to thank the Division of Intercollegiate Athletics, Tom Porter, associate director of athletics, the Division of Campus Recreation, and Ben McGuire, associate director, for sponsoring Medicare for 14 years of tailgates on the west side of Memorial Stadium. Thousands of passers-by, both alumni and football fans, stopped to listen or picnicked in front of the Champaign Park District mobile stage to listen to the music. It was great fun for us, and we hope for those in our audiences. And thanks to all the hard-working secretaries—they really have kept us "honest." With each performance there are at least four to five letters to type and postcards which must be carefully administered and recorded, otherwise we could have two drummers show up for a job or no trumpet player. They also type our tour agendas, make hotel reservations, reserve car rentals and take care of all the nitty-gritty details.

So, from the bottom of our hearts, great big thank-yous to Susan Rose, Medicare's very first secretary who now lives in Kentucky; to Veronica Livesay of Orlando, Florida; to Dorothy Smith, retired in Tempe, Arizona; to Janet Manning, of the School of Music in Urbana, and to my current secretaries Connie Stull and Carolyn Pater who are regulars with the Alumni Association.

Ted Peterson, retired dean of the College of Communications, and Willard Hansen and Chuck Flynn, Editors Emeritus of the *News-Gazette* for their writings on recording jackets and newspaper articles and for their invaluable support through the years.

As of this writing, our new home is in the Illini Union building with the Alumni Association and with the blessing of its executive director, Lou Liay. We have had an ongoing relationship with the Alumni Association dating back to 1972 when we first performed for an alumni brunch prior to a home football game. Since then we have had a close association with this university sponsor, traveling under its banner to 35 states. Of the 79 existing alumni clubs in the nation, we have performed for 51; and of the 17 in the state of Illinois, we have performed for 14. Tentative plans for the 1993-94 year include visits to our 36th and 37th states in the Union.

We are flattered that the Alumni Association invites us to be part of the initiation of new Illini clubs. And, of course, we are grateful to the Association for its interest in us and its willingness to sponsor us on these tours. We have enjoyed those staff members who have served as "chaperones" on the road, including Don Dodds, director of the Urbana campus; Jim Vermette, former executive director of the Association; Patrick Hayes, director of programs and services at Urbana; and, of course, the present CEO, Lou Liay.

We also are pleased when U. of I. Foundation staff members join us on these ventures—Bernie Freeman, Chris Frye and executive director, Bill Nugent, who often sits in with us as a performing member of Medicare. When Bill was a student at North Texas University, along with Morgan Powell, they performed with a Dixieland group called "The Cell Block Seven."

And our thanks to author Nancy Gilmore, whom I knew was already extremely busy with her full-time responsibilities as managing editor of *Illinois Quarterly*. Yet, she accepted the challenge, and what a treat it has been for us. We were not sure of the approach she would use to pull all of this together, but she picked around and probed and kept after me, digging here and there, and even traveled with us on some gigs. And, voila! A most interesting and easy-to-read documentation of 23 years of Medicare is the result. We love you, Nancy! . . . and, thanks!

Finally, my thanks to both John O'Connor, Morris Carter, and Stan Rahn, who along with yours truly, served as the core of the group, and who did much of the planning for all the Medicare activities. John provided the educational materials for our mini-concerts for children, wrote some arrangements when needed and, in general, was there to serve as a sounding board for whatever.

Stan has been my closest associate and, as you have already read, is "the rock" in the Medicare family. He has served as the official business manager and record keeper for Medicare, as accountant, auditor, and close confidant. On tour, he has proved invaluable by taking care of all of our travel expenses, car rentals, food, hotels, etc. I am indeed grateful to him, for without his careful attention to details, I certainly would be in trouble.

What happens next is your guess. When people ask me about the future of Medicare, how long we expect to be together, my response is that "as long as we are physically able to play our instruments and there is an audience, we will keep going."

What is interesting about all of this is that if we had tried to plan it all, it never would have worked. Therefore, we don't try to change anything. Earlier on I said that without these musicians who make up the Medicare family, none of what has gone on the past 23 years would have happened. There is a second part of that statement. Without you, our listening audience, our alumni, Medicare 7, 8 or 9 simply would not exist.

Daniel J. Perrino

The Players

Meet the musicians of Medicare 7, 8 or 9 . . .

On Clarinet

Frank W. Brown
Tallahassee, FL
Professor of music, Florida State University. Conductor of the
   Capital City Band and leader of his own 18-piece band.

Elton Curry
Brandon, FL
Retired. Also plays the curved soprano saxophone. Former director of bands, Urbana Junior High School and a regular
   member with the Rudy James Dixieland Jazz Band and free-
   lance musician.

Marc Gold (deceased)
Urbana, IL
Former professor of education, U. of I. College of Education,
   specializing in special education and leader of his own jazz
   ensemble in Los Angeles.

John Hutchens
Champaign, IL
Also plays soprano saxophone. Formerly with the Fred Waring
   Orchestra; performed with the Perry Como and Andy Wil-
   liams shows, the Five Eleven Jazz Orchestra and leader of his
   own swing band, The Pocket Big Band.

Carlyle Johnson
Champaign, IL

Also plays soprano saxophone. Music educator, director of bands at Edison Junior High School, Champaign. Performed with the Champaign-Urbana Symphony Orchestra, the Tony Bennett Show and Barnum and Bailey Circus.

Kevin Kizer
Maroa, IL

Also plays soprano saxophone. Performs regularly with Dance Band in the Chicago area and leads his own jazz trio.

Dan Kohut
Champaign, IL

Professor of music education and nationally recognized music educator and textbook author at the U. of I. Performs for traveling shows like the Barnum and Bailey Circus and the Ice Capades.

Jack May
Sun Lakes, AZ

Also plays soprano saxophone. Former owner of a True Value hardware store in Urbana, now retired and performing with the Sun Lakes Dixieland Jazz Band.

Stan Rahn *
Urbana, IL

Also plays saxophone. Business manager and administrator of Medicare 7, 8 or 9. One of the band's founders. Now retired after 36 years with the U. of I. as a student affairs administrator. Also an excellent vocalist.

On Saxophone

Ward Ames (deceased)
Danville, IL

Former president of Tri-Dan, a tool and die plant in Danville.

Joe Lulloff
Okemos, MI
Formerly with the U. of I. school of music. Professor of music at Michigan State University. Teaches saxophone and jazz studies. Concertizes both nationally and internationally as a soloist and with symphony orchestras including the St. Louis Symphony.

Dan Perrino *
Urbana, IL
Leader of Medicare 7, 8 or 9 and one of its founders. Former dean of student programs and services, associate dean of the College of Fine and Applied Arts and professor of music at the U. of I. Now with the U. of I. Alumni Association.

Joe Staidlin
Address unknown. Former educator in Rantoul, IL.

On Trumpet/Cornet

Fred Baker
Champaign, IL
Coordinator of the packaging division, Kraft General Foods, Champaign. Played with small combos and large bands in the Champaign-Urbana area.

Bob Bock
Keshena, WI
Retired. Played on the Chesterfield radio show and in bands around the Chicago area. Former All State insurance agent. Now performing with the Firehouse Jazz Band.

Rich Bendle
Chicago, IL
Free-lance musician, playing in Chicago with Jazz Show Case, Andy's, and other jazz spots in the Windy City.

Tom Birkner
Champaign, IL

Assistant professor of music, head of U. of I. jazz studies. Has performed with Members Jazz Band, Nancy Wilson, Joe Williams and the Pocket Big Band. Also vocalist.

Gregg Helgesen
Champaign, IL

Clinical psychologist with Carle Clinic and Hospital. Adjunct professor with the College of Education and faculty member in the School of Medicine. Played with Rudy James' Dixieland Jazz Band and the Pocket Big Band.

Jeff Helgesen
Urbana, IL

Son of Gregg Helgeson and a university jazz band soloist. Performed with the Ray Charles Band for four years, the Jazz Members Big Band, the Pocket Big Band, Anthony Braxton Band, and leads his own combo. Said, "Medicare provided me with my first opportunity to perform jazz in public and was an early influence in my decision to pursue a career as a performing musician."

John O'Connor *
Champaign, IL

Retired. One of original founders of Medicare. Former professor of music/continuing education at the U. of I. Continues to be active with the Jimmy Dorsey Band, Barnum and Bailey Circus, Ice Capades, Orrin Tucker, Champaign-Urbana Symphony Orchestra and with the National Jazz Educators Association.

Russ Pence
Champaign, IL

Vice president of marketing, Research Press. Former music educator. Performed with the Russ Carlyle Orchestra, Rudy James Dixieland Jazz Band and the Don Heitler and Woodward Jazz ensembles.

Raymond Sasaki
Urbana, IL
Professor of music, U. of I. School of Music. Member of the North
 Texas Big Band, recorded for Hollywood movies. Recitalist,
 clinician; performs with the Tone Road Ramblers, the St. Louis
 Brass Quintet and a contemporary ensemble, Team Concept.

On Trombone

Morris Carter *
Urbana, IL
Retired professor of music and assistant director of the School of
 Music. One of the original founders of Medicare. Has per-
 formed in big bands including a short stay with Glenn Miller,
 with the Dick Cisne Orchestra and Mendel Riley Orchestra.

Sean Flanigan
Oak Park, IL
Director of bands at Winston Campus Middle School in Palatine,
 IL. Performed with the U. of I. Jazz Band and trombonist and
 vocalist in the Chicago area.

Mike Gabriel
Champaign, IL
Researcher and professor of biology and psychology at the U. of
 I. Beckman Institute. Has performed with jazz ensembles in
 Wisconsin, Texas, Pennsylvania, and California, with the
 Boneyard ensemble, with Cat Anderson, Tony Ortega, Buddy
 Savit, and Larry McKenna.

Bobby Havens
Simi Valley, CA
A guest performer on several occasions and a regular for more
 than 20 years with the Lawrence Welk Orchestra.

Harvey Hodges
Champaign, IL
Retired realtor and instructor in real estate. In earlier days was an
 active performer with big bands in the Champaign-Urbana
 area.

Alan Horney
Charleston, IL
Professor of music at Eastern Illinois University;Director of jazz
    studies at EIU. A composer, arranger, and conductor.

Britta Langsjoen
New York, NY
U. of I. graduate in chemical engineering and one of the youngest
    members ever to perform with Medicare. Currently seeking
    a career on the professional jazz scene in New York City.

Paul Karlstrom
Champaign, IL
Attorney at law, adjunct professor of law at the U. of I., semi-
    retired. Former leader of his own dance band in the
    Champaign-Urbana area in the late '30s, '40s and '50s.

Erik Lund
Urbana, IL
Professor of music in the U. of I. School of Music. Composer,
    arranger, conductor.

Jerry Martin
Marseilles, IL
Art teacher in the Marseilles school system. Performs with the
    Hirsch-Saunders All Stars and in jazz festivals in the Midwest
    and California. Plans to retire from teaching in 1993 to devote
    full time to playing jazz. Also plays string bass.

Bob Norman
Tucson, AZ
Retired stock broker and leader of his own dance band in the
    Champaign-Urbana area for many years. Also vocalist.

Paul Olson
Glenview, IL
Attorney at law in the Chicago area where he is also an active
    musical performer. Joined Medicare during Dads Day week-
    end on campus when his son and daughter were university
    students.

Bob Parkinson
Hobe Sound, FL
Retired chief executive officer of Research Press in Champaign. Former performer with the Bob Strong Dance Band and Rudy James Dixieland Band.

Morgan Powell
Tuscola, IL
Professor of music composition in the U. of I. School of Music. An active composer of "new music" with many compositions and awards to his credit. Performed with the North Texas Big Band, the Cell Block Seven Dixieland Band, the Tone Road Ramblers, the Boneyard Band, and the Rudy James Dixieland Band. On the faculty of the Stan Kenton School of Jazz.

James Priebe
Address unknown
Music educator

Robert Schaefer (deceased)
Formerly with the Office of Music Extension and Illinois Summer Youth Music. Leader of his own big band, arranger and historian of big band music recordings and stories.

John Sexton
Ganado, AZ
Music educator and band director for the Navajo Indian schools in New Mexico. Played with the U. of I. Jazz Band and small jazz combos in the Champaign-Urbana area.

Barry Wagner
Urbana, IL
Facilities manager with the Fire Service Institute at the U. of I. Leader of his own Firehouse Five-Eleven Jazz Orchestra and a regular with the Beverly Wolfe Ensemble.

On Piano

Phil Ahern
Houston, TX
Composer. Performed with the Rudy James Dixieland Jazz Band.

Hank Cahill
Champaign, IL
Retired. Part owner of the Piano People. Former executive in
    industry, member of the Columbus Symphony Orchestra
    and an active performer with dance bands in the Champaign-
    Urbana area.

Dick Cisne (deceased)
Urbana, IL
Well-known leader of his own dance orchestra which was the
    first to perform in the Illini Union building in 1941. A signifi-
    cant number of Medicare members have played with the
    Cisne orchestra, which began in 1929 and continued until his
    death in the late '70s.

Mike Dunn
New Jersey
Former professor of classics at the U. of I. Free-lance musician in
    the New York area.

Larry Dwyer *
South Bend, IN
An original member of the Medicare band at its first performance
    in 1969 and a U. of I. graduate student at the time. An
    accomplished rag time pianist who performed with the U. of
    I. Jazz Band as a trombonist.

Bill French
Champaign, IL
Also plays drums. A faculty member at Parkland College,
    Champaign, and teacher in the public schools. Performed
    with the Steve Allen Show and others.

Don Heitler
Urbana, IL

Full-time musician/performer, arranger and writer. Has recorded with George Shearing and Urbie Green. Performed at the London House and Mr. Kelly's in Chicago, and at the Sahara and the Top of the Mint in Las Vegas with the American Music Trio. Collaborator with Professor James Lyke in arranging piano music for intermediate and adult piano students. Publisher, Columbia Pictures.

Mike Kocour
Kenilworth, IL

Jazz pianist in the Chicago area. Instructor of piano at the U. of I. and Northwestern University. Performs with the American Music Trio.

Verne Kuetmeyer (deceased)
Monticello, IL

Former music educator in Monticello, Ill., and an active performer in dance bands in the area.

John Leslie
Riverside, IL

Retired music educator. Active performer in hotels and clubs in the Chicago area.

Rick Murphy
Champaign, IL

Instructor of music at University High School, Urbana. Active solo pianist in the area.

Bill Nugent
Champaign, IL

Executive Director, U. of I. Foundation. Performed with the Cell Block Seven Dixieland Band in Texas. Also performed in Las Vegas and on the Ed Sullivan Show. A concert pianist and conductor and adjunct professor in the U. of I. School of Music.

Ron Riddle
Sarasota, FL

Head of the humanities division of the University of South
Florida. Musicologist and superb rag time pianist who has
concertized across the nation.

Armand Tosetti
Decatur, IL

Retired. Played professionally in Chicago at the Drake Hotel,
Chez Paree, Capitol Lounge, the Brass Rail and the Blue Note.
Performed with Dick Jurgens, Eddie Howard and the Monty
Mountjoy Dixieland group.

Gordon Wilson
Urbana, IL

Owner of his own keyboard studio. Has performed as a soloist in
clubs and hotels, with the Celebration and Fine and Mellow
Bands. Director of music at the Grace Methodist Church
choir, Urbana.

Charles Winking (deceased)
Quincy, IL

Former director, music department, Quincy College. Was an
active jazz musician in western Illinois and leader of his own
jazz band.

Woody Woodward
Urbana, IL

Professor of biology, physiology and anatomy at Parkland College, Champaign. Leader of his own jazz ensemble and at one
time, a Latin jazz ensemble. Radio disk jockey and active
pianist in the Champaign-Urbana area.

George Shearing
New York, NY

Guest performer with Medicare in the early years.

On String Bass/Tuba

Pete Bridgewater (string bass)
Urbana, IL

Retired after 30 years with the U. of I. Played professionally in the Midwest as leader of his own jazz combo; DJ with his own jazz radio show on WDWS for 20 years and, in recent years, on WBCP.

Jim Cox (string bass)
Skokie, IL

He is a full-time professional playing in Chicago with the Judy Roberts Trio, Marian McPartland, at the Nikko Hotel, Andy's Jazz Club and other shows in the Windy City area. Joined Medicare while an undergraduate at the U. of I.

Adam Davis
Champaign, IL

Presently an undergraduate student in the U. of I. School of Music and top bassist in the jazz division. Free lances in the area with the Pocket Big Band and other jazz groups.

Glen Dewey (string bass)
Decatur, IL

Professor of music at Milliken University, associate principal with the Springfield Symphony Orchestra and the Illinois Chamber Orchestra, free lance musician with jazz, rock, Dixieland and other shows throughout the Midwest.

Dan DeLorenzo
Chicago, IL

Free-lance musician in the Chicago area performing at Andy's Jazz Club and other jazz spots in the Midwest.

Hank Feldman (tuba)
Tucson, AZ

Associate director of bands and professor of tuba at the University of Arizona. Soloist and clinician. Joined Medicare while a graduate student at the U. of I.

Warren Felts
Aurora, IL
Retired after 30 years of teaching and directing bands in Illinois, 35 of those years as director of bands at West Aurora High School. His sole desire after retirement was to play jazz in New Orleans. Became a regular on the streets and in the jazz clubs in New Orleans and performed with Al Hirt, Pete Fountain, George Shearing and Mel Torme. Played in Preservation Hall, on the Mississippi Queen and Delta Queen, at funerals, and at jazz festivals in France, Colombia, Mexico and in San Francisco. Currently a regular with the Connie Jones Crescent City Jazz Band.

Terry Gates
Buffalo, NY
Former director of music at Muskingham College, Muskingham, Ohio.

John Hurtubise
Chicago, IL
Computer engineer in Chicago; free-lance musician performing in jazz clubs in Chicago.

David James
Columbia, MO
Instructor at the University of Missouri. Performs with bands in the area.

Fritz Kaenzig (tuba)
Ann Arbor, MI
Former professor of tuba at the U. of I. School of Music; currently at the University of Michigan. Concert artist and performer with the Detroit and St. Louis Symphony orchestras, the Michigan Opera Theater and principal tuba player with the Grant Park Symphony Orchestra, Chicago. He has said, "Playing with Medicare has been one of the most enjoyable experiences in my musical career. I'll forever remember playing 'Asleep in the Deep' at a Halloween concert wearing a werewolf mask."

Karen Korsemeyer Randolla (string bass)
New York, NY

Currently completing her MBA degree at New York University and is vice president of information management with United Way of Westchester, N.Y. Free-lance musician. Has worked with the Kit McClure Big Band which recently performed at the Clinton presidential inauguration in Washington, D.C. Has toured with the band in Europe and Japan.

Viktor Krauss (string bass)
Nashville, TN

Free-lance musician in Nashville. Has performed with sister Allison, a two-time Grammy Award winner. While in the Champaign-Urbana area, played with a variety of jazz ensembles including the Woody Woodward Trio.

Ross Martin (deceased) (gut bucket)
Urbana, IL

Former associate dean in charge of research in the U. of I. College of Engineering. Performed with Medicare for student concerts during the '60s and '70s.

John Pennell
Urbana, IL

Free-lance musician performing with a variety of ensembles in the C-U area. Formerly with the Allison Krauss Blue Grass Ensemble and composer of the 1993 Grammy Award-winning song for Krauss. Also composed other songs for the Krauss blue grass group.

Dan Perantoni (tuba)
Chandler, AZ

Former professor of tuba at the U. of I. School of Music. Currently with the school of music at Arizona State University. Soloist and clinician. Performs with the St. Louis Brass Quintet and the Summit Brass. Has made recordings with a variety of brass ensembles. Former performer with the Tuba Jazz Consort and one of the earlier members of Medicare.

Don Percival (string bass)
Nashville, IN

Former professor of wood technology with the Small Homes Council of the U. of I. School of Architecture. Performed with the Salty Dogs while on the Purdue University campus. Performed with the Rudy James Orchestra in C-U.

Paul Rainey (string bass and tuba)
Villa Park, IL

Coordinator of the Data Process Center with the Elmhurst School District #205. Formerly with the Johnny Bruce and Al Pierson dance bands. He is a recording engineer.

Mike Richardson (string bass and tuba)
Chesterfield, MO

Minister of music with the Bonhomme Presbyterian Church in Chesterfield. Music director with both the Bel Canto Chorus of St. Louis and the Great American People Show, Springfield, Ill. An active soloist, arranger and composer of choral music.

Fred Trevarthan (string bass)
Urbana, IL

New performer with Medicare. Free lances in the C-U area.

On Drums

Steve Adleman
Champaign, IL

Student at Parkland College majoring in jazz studies. Free-lance musician.

Don Baker
San Francisco, CA

Ph.D. in percussion from the U. of I. Studied percussion and performed in West Africa. Teaches and performs in San Francisco. Director of the Music Camp at the San Mateo Community College.

Allen Bates (traps, vibes and steel drum)
New York, NY
Free-lance musician in New York. Performed with big bands in
    Japan and for several years in the Virgin Islands. Presently
    continuing his education in Japanese studies at New York
    University.

Steve Beck
Lawton, OK
Director, International Percussive Arts Society. Performs with
    the Lawton (Okla.) Symphony Orchestra and free lances in
    the area.

Laurence Beers
Address unknown

Charles Braugham *
Chicago, IL
Self-employed musician: "Wherever the phone calls take me."
    Has performed primarily in New York and Chicago but also
    on the road with jazz units at nationally prominent festivals;
    toured with Elvis Presley and recently performed with Rose-
    mary Clooney, Marian McPartland, at Andy's Jazz Club, the
    Cotton Club and with the house band at the Fairmount Hotel
    in Chicago.

John Bromley
Danville, IL
Doctor of optometry and an active performer in eastern Illinois
    with big bands and small jazz combos. A regular with the
    Firehouse Five-Eleven Jazz Orchestra. Director of the nation-
    ally known Sports Vision program and an active lecturer and
    clinician for coaches of athletic teams across the country.

Bruce Doctor
New York, NY
Performing in New York in "pit" orchestras on Broadway and
    Off Broadway shows.

Michael Friedman
Address unknown
Last heard was performing as a free-lance musician in the Chicago area.

Phil Gratteau
Chicago, IL
Free-lance musician in Chicago performing with the Judy Roberts Trio, Eddie Johnson, Eric Schneider, Richie Cole, "Made in Brazil," and at Andy's Jazz Club. Has recorded with Joe Henderson and Akio Sasajima. Teaches at Roosevelt University.

Bill Gray
Champaign, IL
Manager and partner of "The Music Shop." Leader of his own jazz ensemble and promoter of jazz groups in the Midwest.

Roger Holmes
Springfield, IL
Judge of the Seventh Judicial Court in the state of Illinois. Active with several community theater groups in the Springfield area. Serves on the board of the Springfield Muni-Opera Company.

Rudy James
Champaign, IL
Retired musician, band leader and long-time officer of the AFM Local 196 and booking agent. His Dixieland band served as a nucleus of that style of jazz in the area.

Kent Johnson
Champaign, IL
Technical writer for CSC Intelicom in Champaign-Urbana. Performs with a variety of jazz units and fusion bands.

Kevin Krall
Chicago, IL
Free-lance musician in Chicago. Works in the electronics industry.

John Leister
Farwood, NJ
Music educator in the Farwood schools. Free-lance musician in
the New Jersey and New York area.

Maurice McKinley
New York, NY
Teacher with the Boys Choir of Harlem. Director of his own
production company, "Three Sisters Music." Free-lance musician in New York City.

John Meyers
Jersey City, NJ
Free-lance musician in New York and New Jersey. Performs in
Broadway and Off Broadway shows and with the Vince
Giardinos' Nighthawks.

Ken Palmer (deceased)
Champaign, IL
Former active performer with dance bands in the C-U area.

Dave Parkinson
Redwood City, CA
Self-employed and owner of his own firm; printing broker.
Retired from performance.

Dave Roberts
Address unknown
Last known address was in the Denver, CO area.

Dick Selander (deceased)
Urbana, IL
Former professor of entomology and physiology at the U. of I.

Joel Spencer
Chicago, IL
Free-lance musician in Chicago, performing and recording with
named jazz greats and with a variety of jazz ensembles; Jazz
Show Case and Andy's Jazz Club. On the faculty at De Paul
University teaching percussion.

Jeff Stitely
Chicago, IL
Leader of his own jazz ensemble in Chicago. Active performer with a variety of jazz groups including Andy's Jazz Club.

Bob Towner
Urbana, IL
Leader of his own band, Celebration. Performs for dances, shows, parties. Coordinator of transportation with the Lincoln Trails Library system. Versatile musician who can perform country, rock and jazz.

Dean "Bucky" Wade
Washington, D.C.
Program manager, Soza and Co., Ltd., Falls Church, Va. Associate conductor, National Concert Band of America.

Dennis Wiziecki
Urbana, IL
Advertising manager, Research Press Publishing Co., Champaign. Percussion instructor at the Conservatory of Central Illinois. Free-lance musician. Active volunteer with music department at Urbana High School.

Brad Woodward
Urbana, IL
Warehouse manager, Research Press Publishing Co. Youngest drummer with Medicare and "doing well."

On Banjo

Gene Adams (string bass, jazz violin and guitar)
Bryan, TX
Retired. Former music educator in the Quincy and Danville, Ill., schools. A symphonic and jazz musician.

Thad Bales
Chicago, IL
He is in the engineering business.

Stan Icenogle
Cody, WY
Former football player with the Fighting Illini. Not a trained
musician but a "whale of a Dixieland jazz banjoist."

Jordan Kaye (string bass and guitar)
Pesotum, IL
Free-lance musician in the area. Leader of his own jazz ensemble.
An instructor in the Urbana Adult Education Program of
country and blue grass music.

John O'Brien
Springfield, VA
Performed with the Rudy James Dixieland Jazz Band and served
as a musician with the Chanute Field Air Force Band.

Art Proteau *
Clearwater, FL
Served as the only banjoist during the early days of Medicare.
Also performed with the Bill Donahue and Dick Cisne Or-
chestras and was a vocalist remembered for such oldies as
"Minnie the Mermaid" and "Peeking Through the Knot Hole
of Father's Wooden Leg."

Earle Roberts
Danville, IL
"Youngest" member of the Medicare family who turned 92 on
July 26, 1993. A regular with vaudeville shows in Chicago as
early as 1919. Performed with NBC radio orchestra and on
the Don McNeil Breakfast Club.

On Guitar

Terry Bradds
Urbana, IL
Senior minister at the Webber Street Church of Christ, Urbana.
When time is available, he plays a "mean" jazz guitar.

Donald Perrino
Urbana, IL
Performed with the jazz rock group, "All Star Frogs." Presently
  inactive.

Gene Wilder
Champaign, IL
The first guitarist to play with Medicare.

Vocalists

Phyllis Denny
Urbana, IL
Sang with the Johnny Renaldo Swing Band in the '50s and also in
  jazz clubs with the Don Heitler Group and the Woody
  Woodward Trio.

Nancy Hays
Chicago, IL
Country Western and top 40 singer and recording artist in Las
  Vegas. Has performed with shows across the nation. Nancy
  sang with Medicare while still an undergraduate student at
  the U. of I.

Annie Helgesen
Champaign, IL
Currently a student at Illinois Wesleyan University, Bloomington,
  majoring in communications.

Jeff Humphrey
Champaign, IL
Retired. Formerly with the U. of I. Housing Division.

Alison Krauss
Nashville, TN
Guest vocalist with Medicare and a 1991 and 1993 Grammy
  Award winner.

Rachel Lee
Springfield, IL
Free-lance vocalist performing in the Chicago area at the Cotton Club, Andy's Jazz Club, the Chicago Jazz Festival in Grant Park, at Comiskey Park (home of the Chicago White Sox) and teaches commercial vocal styles at Milliken University.

Harry Ruedi
Urbana, IL
Retired. A Jolson-style singer who performed in clubs in the early days in Chicago. Was a haberdasher for 45 years, primarily with Hart Shaffner and Marx. Still sings, but for his 12 grandchildren.

George Staley
Address unknown
Was an active vocalist in New York City.

Dena Vermette
Champaign, IL
Free-lance vocalist who performs in jazz clubs in the C-U area with Don Heitler and Woody Woodward; also a special-function entertainer.

* Original members of Medicare 7, 8 or 9

Note: Apologies to those musicians who have played with the band at some time or another but who are not listed here. Our record keeping, without clerical staff to keep up on such matters of complete accuracy, prevents us from doing so. —D.P.

Bringing People Together

The following is a partial list of groups that Medicare 7, 8 or 9 has entertained over the years.

University of Illinois Alumni Association
Illini Club Programs (53 out of a total of 79 nationally)
Alumni Association Recognition Dinners
Illinois State Fair Program
Annual Alumni Reunions on the Urbana Campus
Cubs-Cardinals Baseball Games
University Foundation Day

Illini Union Building (Urbana)
Mini concerts in the North and South Lounges
Performances for Illini Union Staff

Illini Union Building (Chicago)
College of Medicine

Levis Faculty Center Open House

Conferences, Workshops, Symposia, Short Courses
On Campus
Cooperative Extension Service - College of Agriculture
International Symposium of Liquid/Solid Waste
Livestock Wastes Symposium
Grain Dealers Conference
Rural Policy Forum
Future Farmers Leadership Conference

Savings and Loan Short Courses
National Collegiate Athletic Association
Estate Planning Short Courses
Illinois Fruit Council
Illinois Teaching Association
Illinois Nursing Home Association
Arborculturist Council
College of Agriculture and Departments
College of Education and Departments
College of Engineering and Departments
College of Commerce and Departments
College of Liberal Arts and Sciences and Departments
College of Applied Life Studies and Departments
School of Architecture Awards Night

Off Campus
National Council for the Aging
Midwest Governors Conference
Illinois State Musicians Union
District Exchange Conference
District Lions Club Conference
District Rotary Club Conference
Illinois Bar Association Conference
Illinois State Secretarial Conference

Orientation Programs
Illinois State University Student Association
University of Illinois Quad Day, Residence Halls, Fraternities   and
    Sororities
U. of I. College of Law
U. of I. School of Art and Design
Illinois Music Educators
U. of I. College of Medicine, Peoria

Concerts
U. of I. Star Course
Krannert Center for the Performing Arts
First National Bank Plaza, Chicago
Chicago Daley Plaza
College of Medicine, Rockford
Lincoln Trails College, Robinson
Wabash Valley College, Marshall
Spoon River College, Canton
Central College, Olney

Rend Lake College
Lakeland College, Mattoon
Quincy College
Southeastern College, Harrisburg
DuPage Community College
Herrin Community Concert Series
Greater Alton Community
Mt. Prospect Community
Continuing Education, District 88 Benefit (20 years running)
George Burns Show, U. of I. Assembly Hall
United Way, U. of I. Assembly Hall
California Institute of Technology
Central Illinois Children's Chorus
Statewide Concerts for Elementary, Middle and High Schools
Regional and National Music Education Conferences in Milwaukee, Los Angeles, Chicago, St. Louis
Symphony Orchestras in Champaign-Urbana, Quincy, Decatur, and Green Bay, Wis.
Concert and Symphonic Band Performances at the University of Illinois, Danville Community College and Wheaton College
Park Districts—Champaign, Urbana, Decatur, St. Joseph, Homer, Rockford, Peoria, Quincy, Belleville, Chicago, Wheaton

Athletic Events
Tailgates Prior to Illinois Football Games (14 years)
Half-time Shows with the Marching Illini Band
U. of I. Basketball Games
U. of I. Women's Gymnastics Competitions
U. of I. Women's Volleyball Games
U. of I. Golf Outings—Grants-In-Aid Program
Rose Bowl
Liberty Bowl
Illinois-Stanford Football Game

Churches
For Methodists, Presbyterian, Baptist, Catholic, United Church of Christ, Episcopal, Lutheran — in the Champaign-Urbana area, around the state of Illinois and out of state

Retirements
Chancellor Jack Peltason
Chancellor Tom Everhart
More than 50 Faculty Members and U. of I. Staff
Government Leaders, including Gov. Dan Walker of Illinois
Gen. Norman Brown, Commanding Officer of Chanute Field

Memorial Services and Funerals

Parades
Fourth of July Parade, Champaign-Urbana

Miscellaneous
U. of I. Panhellenic Council
U. of I. Campus Secretariat (16 years)
U. of I. Clerical Association
Busey Bank Corn Festival, Urbana
Varsity "I" Men's Banquet
Foundation for Excellence in Education
Covenant Hospital Hospice, Urbana
Illinois Arts Council
U. of I. Dads Association
U. of I. Mothers Association
Air Force Society, Chanute Air Force Base, Rantoul
Carle Foundation
Illinois State Fair—Senior Citizens
Paxton Chamber of Commerce
Illinois Parks and Recreation
Quincy River Festival
Illinois State Chamber of Commerce
Nursing Homes
Retirement Homes
Hospitals
Shopping Centers
Arts Festivals
Elderhouses
Opening of Willard Airport
"Empty Tomb" Award Banquet
Robeson's Department Store
Chicago Cultural Center, Office of the Mayor
American Institute of Architects
Chicago Bears—St. Louis Cardinals Football Games
American Association of Retired People
Covenant Hospital Auxiliary
Bell Telephone— Peoria, Springfield, Elmhurst, Joliet
Illinois Fire Chiefs Association Conference
U. of I. Police Institute
Illinois Association of College and University Staffing
Illinois Health Fairs, U. of I. and Eastern Illinois University